THE COGNITIVE ATHLETE

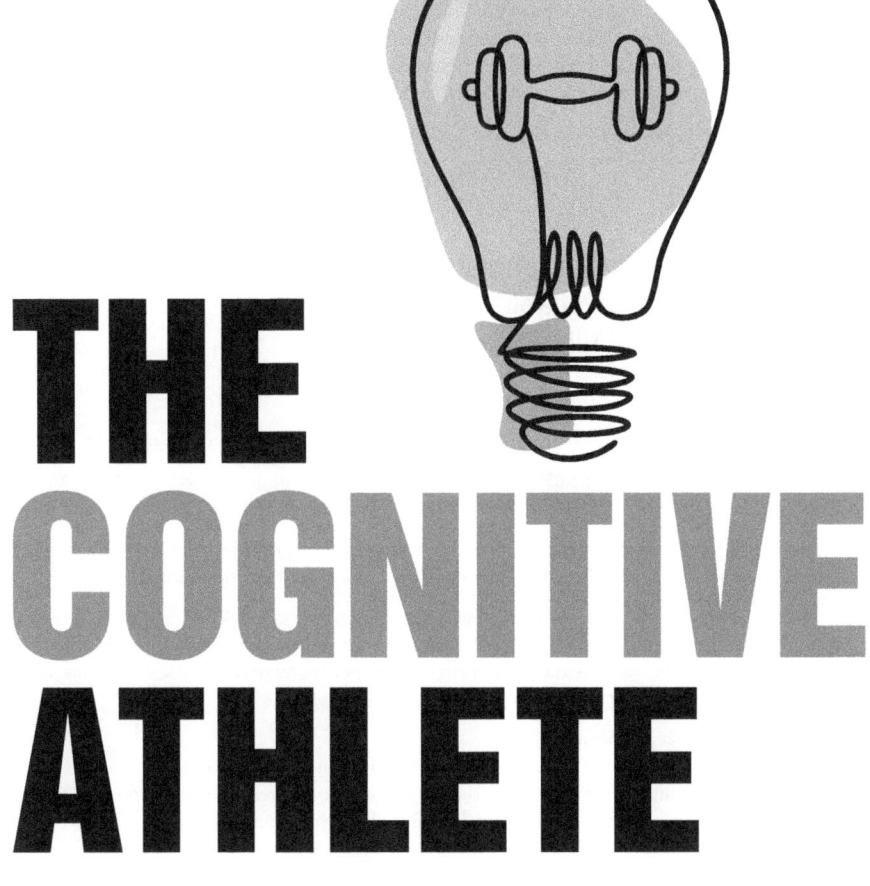

THE COGNITIVE ATHLETE

Sustainable Peak Performance for Leaders, Thinkers and Doers

Clint Rahe

WILEY

First published 2026 by John Wiley & Sons Australia, Ltd

ISBN: 978-1-394-37537-0

A catalogue record for this book is available from the National Library of Australia

Registered Office
John Wiley & Sons Australia, Ltd. Level 4, 600 Bourke Street, Melbourne, VIC 3000, Australia

For details of our global editorial offices, customer services, and more information about Wiley products visit us at www.wiley.com.

Wiley also publishes its books in a variety of electronic formats and by print-on-demand. Some content that appears in standard print versions of this book may not be available in other formats.

Cover design by Wiley
Cover Images: © Anettestock/Adobe Stock; © MdIkramul/Adobe Stock

Set in 12/15pts and Crimson Text by Straive, Chennai, India.
Printed and bound by CPI Group (UK) Ltd, Croydon, CR0 4YY

C9781394375370_051225

The manufacturer's authorized representative according to the EU General Product Safety Regulation is Wiley-VCH GmbH, Boschstr. 12, 69469 Weinheim, Germany, e-mail: Product_Safety@wiley.com.

To Emma — thank you for being the calm in the chaos, the one who steadies me when I lose focus, and the voice of reason when doubt creeps in. You're the beat!

And to Ella and Harrison — for always keeping me on my toes and reminding me what really matters.

Contents

About the Author

Clint Rahe is a speaker, facilitator and high-performance coach specialising in cognitive performance. He works with professionals, leaders and teams to optimise energy, sharpen focus and build resilience, ensuring sustainable success in high-pressure environments.

Clint began his military career as a Physical Training Instructor in the Royal Air Force (RAF), where he trained fast-jet pilots and personnel preparing for operations in the Middle East. This role exposed him to working with elite athletes and professional sports teams, applying the principle of periodisation, peaking at the right time for competition or deployment.

As his career progressed, Clint qualified as an Adventurous Training Instructor, using activities such as rock climbing, mountaineering and canoeing/kayaking as powerful mediums for professional and team development. These controlled environments allowed leaders, small operational units and special forces to experience high-pressure situations that prepared them physically and mentally for the rigours of battle. This combination of physical conditioning and mental preparation reinforced his belief that sustainable high performance requires both.

Upon leaving the RAF, Clint returned to his native Australia and pursued a corporate career. Very quickly he recognised a gap: the same level of training, preparation and execution that defined elite military and sporting performance was missing in business. Just as soldiers who skipped preparation were more likely to falter under pressure, he saw professionals burning out and underperforming for lack of structured training and recovery. Out of this realisation, he began developing the Corporate Athlete framework, the foundation that would evolve into *The Cognitive Athlete*.

For more than 20 years since, Clint has translated these principles into leadership programs and coaching pathways for executives, entrepreneurs, and high-performing teams across industries. His approach blends sports science, neuroscience and behavioural psychology into practical tools that help professionals manage pressure, recover effectively, and sustain peak performance.

Today, as a speaker and facilitator, Clint has worked with leading organisations worldwide, delivering workshops and executive coaching that transform how individuals and teams approach performance, recovery and resilience.

Clint lives in Sydney, Australia, with his wife and two children. He coaches youth soccer and athletics, volunteers as a patrolling member of Surf Life Saving NSW on the Central Coast, spends time on the water and road-tests his own performance frameworks in daily life.

The Cognitive Athlete is his first book, a playbook for building unshakeable focus, resilience, and sustainable high performance in today's demanding world.

INTRODUCTION
The modern professional's dilemma

It's Tuesday morning, and Dawn is already behind. As the head of a business unit in a global financial firm, her day begins at 6 am, responding to emails from her team in the United States. She scrambles through breakfast, juggling tasks on her phone while half-listening to the morning news in the background. She's barely had time to sip her coffee before she's pulled into the day's first crisis — an urgent client issue that needs her immediate attention. A message from her boss flashes across her screen: *Can you jump on a quick call?* The request isn't really a question; it's an expectation. Dawn sighs, grabs her laptop and settles in for another relentless day.

By 9 am, she's in back-to-back meetings with her Australian colleagues, barely able to focus on one discussion before being pulled into the next. The conversations blur together, mixing performance reports with budget reviews and project deadlines. Somewhere between the third and fourth Teams call, she realises she hasn't taken a single deep breath.

By noon, she's running on caffeine and adrenaline. Eating at her desk has become the norm, and skipping lunch completely isn't uncommon.

She quickly types out responses to urgent emails between calls, knowing that if she doesn't reply now, they'll pile up even further.

Her to-do list is growing faster than she can clear it.

By 3 pm, her energy starts to dip, but there's no time to rest. More emails, more meetings. An unexpected request from senior leadership throws her entire schedule into chaos, forcing her to reshuffle priorities once again. She had planned to spend the afternoon on deep work, but now she's putting out fires and reacting instead of strategising.

By 6 pm, Dawn finally steps away from her laptop and leaves her home office, heading into the kitchen where her family is already gathered. Rushing through dinner, she listens half-heartedly as her kids excitedly talk about their day, but her mind is still stuck on unanswered emails and the tasks she hasn't finished. Her phone sits next to her plate, lighting up every few minutes with notifications she tries to ignore.

By 7 pm, she's helping with the bedtime routine of bathing the kids, reading a short story and tucking them in. She knows she should be more present, but her attention drifts. As her youngest asks for one more hug, she feels a pang of guilt. *I should spend more time with them,* she thinks, *but there's just too much to do.*

By 8 pm, the house is quiet, and she has a brief moment to breathe. She considers unwinding with her husband, maybe watching a show together, but the pull of unfinished work is too strong. She grabs her laptop to clear out a few more emails before her next round of meetings.

By 10 pm, she's back in her home office, logging in for meetings with her European colleagues. Her eyes are heavy, her focus fading, but skipping these calls isn't an option. Decisions need to be made, reports need to be reviewed and expectations remain high. She forces herself to stay engaged, nodding along as her team discusses strategy, but her mind feels sluggish, struggling to process information as quickly as usual.

By 12 am, the meetings finally wrap up. She shuts her laptop and steps away from her desk, exhausted but unable to relax. Even as she climbs into bed, her mind won't switch off. She mentally runs through the next day's schedule — an early client meeting, two strategy sessions and a performance review. Sleep doesn't come easy.

The next morning, it all starts again.

The cost of constant overload

Dawn is proud of her work ethic. She's always been someone who pushes through challenges, meets deadlines and takes ownership. She has built her career on being the person who never drops the ball. But, deep down, she knows something is wrong.

She's exhausted all the time. No matter how early she goes to bed, she wakes up feeling drained and as if she hasn't rested at all. The brain fog is creeping in, and tasks that once felt effortless now take twice as long. She stares at her screen, struggling to process emails that should take seconds to read. The simplest decisions — such as what to eat, what to wear, whether she has time to work out — feel overwhelming.

Her body is showing signs of stress, too. A simple cold that used to pass in a few days now lingers for weeks. She finds herself getting sick more often, and catching every flu and virus going around. Headaches are now a regular part of her day, and she's relying on caffeine and painkillers to keep functioning. Her digestion is off, and she can't remember the last time she felt truly well.

But the worst part is that the moment she finally gets a break, her body completely shuts down.

Every year, she looks forward to taking annual leave. She pictures herself on the beach with her family, sleeping in and waking up feeling refreshed. But as soon as she finally steps away from work, exhaustion hits her like a freight train. On her first day off, she feels unusually tired.

By the second day, she's in bed with a pounding headache, body aches and a sore throat. What was supposed to be a time to recharge turns into a week of lying in bed, feeling miserable, frustrated and defeated.

She spends the entire year pushing through exhaustion, only to spend her hard-earned time off recovering. Instead of enjoying her break, she spends it feeling run-down. By the end, she has recovered just enough to crawl back into the chaos and start the cycle all over again.

Dawn feels disconnected from the things that used to bring her joy. She used to love exercising, but now she can't find the energy. She used to enjoy reading, but she's too mentally drained to focus on a book. Even her time with her family feels fragmented. She's physically there, but her mind is somewhere else. Her husband notices she's always distracted. Her kids barely get a full conversation from her before she checks her phone. Even on weekends, she's never fully present.

She's tried using productivity apps, time-blocking and even mindfulness, but nothing sticks. The more she tries to optimise her work, the more depleted she feels.

Dawn's story is not unique.

Millions of professionals find themselves trapped in this relentless forwards motion — always 'on', always chasing impossible expectations and constantly juggling competing priorities. For too many, the pressure to perform has become a silent epidemic, leaving high achievers stretched thin, uninspired and at risk of burnout.

If you've picked up this book, perhaps you feel a lot like Dawn. I'm here to tell you that you can break free from the exhaustion cycle and learn how to achieve excellence without sacrificing wellbeing. It's time to rethink how you work, perform and recover so that success no longer comes at the cost of health and happiness. It's time to thrive rather than just survive.

You don't need to push harder. You need a new way to work. And that's exactly what this book will teach you.

Why are we struggling?

The modern workplace has become an unrelenting environment of high expectations, constant connectivity and overwhelming demands. Many professionals are working longer hours, multitasking endlessly, and sacrificing their health and relationships just to keep up. The result is burnout, chronic stress and a relentless feeling of always being one step behind.

But the problem isn't just the volume of work; it's also the way we approach it. We have been conditioned to believe that success is a direct result of working harder, pushing through exhaustion and constantly being available. We treat ourselves as if we're machines, expecting continual output with minimal downtime, and ignoring the fact that we are biological beings with natural energy cycles that need managing.

This mindset of continual output, born from outdated productivity models, fails to account for the mental, emotional and physical toll of high-pressure environments. Many of us feel the pressure to be 'always on'—answering emails late into the night, responding to Teams messages on weekends and squeezing in 'just one more task' before bed. The line between work and personal life has completely blurred, and for many professionals, true rest feels impossible.

Research consistently shows that burnout is at an all-time high. According to Gallup's 2020 report, *Employee Burnout: Causes and Cures*, for example, nearly 76 per cent of employees report feeling burned out at least some of the time. This is compounded by the 'always-on' culture, driven by technology, which blurs the lines between work and personal time. For leaders and knowledge workers especially, the mental load of decision-making, problem-solving and managing people adds a layer of complexity that's hard to quantify but deeply felt.

The consequences extend far beyond just feeling tired, and include the following:

- *Diminished performance:* Burnout leads to cognitive fatigue, slower decision-making and reduced creativity. In other words, the harder you push, the worse you perform.

- *Emotional exhaustion:* Chronic stress drains emotional resilience, making you more irritable, disengaged, and less effective in leadership and teamwork.

- *Physical health decline:* Long-term stress weakens the immune system, increases the risk of heart disease and contributes to sleep disorders.

- *The let-down effect:* Getting sick the moment you take a break is a clear sign of a system in overdrive.

- *Disengagement and turnover:* Teams with high burnout rates experience low morale, higher turnover and reduced innovation. Companies lose top talent — not because you or your team can't do the job, but because you can't sustain the way you are expected to work.

The modern approach to work is failing you. You're pushing harder, but you're not getting further. Something has to change.

The Cognitive Athlete approach

The solution lies in redefining how you think about performance. In the following chapters, I outline the concept of the Cognitive Athlete — an approach that borrows from the principles of elite sports to help professionals achieve peak mental and emotional performance in a sustainable way. Just as physical athletes train, recover and prepare with purpose, Cognitive Athletes must adopt a structured, intentional approach to managing their mental and emotional resources.

At the heart of this approach is *periodisation*—a method used by elite athletes and military operators to balance intense effort with deliberate recovery. Instead of trying to perform at maximum capacity all the time, you can use periodisation to focus on what matters most, when it matters most. Through this process, you can align work and rest cycles, set boundaries and build resilience to handle high-pressure situations without burning out.

This book guides you through the four key phases of periodisation: Conditioning, Transition, Performance and Recovery. Each phase builds on the previous one, creating a sustainable framework for peak performance. You'll learn how to align your schedule with your natural rhythms, manage mental load and prioritise recovery as a critical part of your success.

The Cognitive Athlete approach isn't about doing more; it's about doing better. By shifting your mindset and adopting these strategies, you'll not only enhance your productivity but also regain balance, focus and joy in your personal and professional life. It's time to stop sprinting through a marathon and start thriving in your role.

Why this book and this approach?

Why should you trust this book? Because it's based on my rigorous research and decades of experience working with people in the most demanding environments — including military operations, elite sports teams and corporate leadership.

As a former Physical Training Instructor in the Royal Air Force, I've seen firsthand the importance of balancing performance with recovery. In the military, we trained soldiers to thrive under extreme pressure while maintaining the resilience needed to adapt and endure. This experience carried over into my work with professional sports teams, where I helped athletes prepare for high-stakes competitions. From endurance training to recovery protocols, I've witnessed the transformative power of structured, intentional preparation. The same principles apply to the corporate world. Over the past decade, I've worked with leaders, teams and organisations to adapt these strategies for professional environments, helping people navigate challenges and achieve their goals without sacrificing their health or happiness.

What makes the Cognitive Athlete approach different is its practicality. This book doesn't rely solely on theory. And it's not about productivity hacks or vague self-help advice. It's a framework rooted in evidence, tailored to the realities of modern work. Whether you're a CEO, entrepreneur, manager or aspiring leader, this book provides actionable strategies you can implement immediately.

You don't need to burn out to succeed. You don't need to choose between your career and your wellbeing. By adopting the Cognitive Athlete mindset, you can achieve sustainable peak performance and unlock a level of resilience and satisfaction you never thought possible. This book is your guide to making it happen.

By the end of this book, you'll have a practical system to:

- train your brain like an elite athlete
- work in structured cycles (periodisation) for peak performance
- achieve more with less stress, fewer hours and greater energy.

You don't have to sacrifice your health, family or happiness to be successful. You just need a better way to work — and this is it.

How to use this book

This book is designed to be a practical guide for achieving sustainable high performance. Whether you're a business leader, entrepreneur, creative professional or knowledge worker, *The Cognitive Athlete* can help you manage your energy, sharpen your focus and prevent burnout, allowing you to perform at your best for the long run.

Unlike traditional productivity books that focus on doing more in less time, this book is about working smarter, not harder. The strategies in the following pages are based on the science of peak performance, periodisation and cognitive endurance. These are the same principles used by elite athletes to sustain excellence without burnout. Now, you can apply these methods to your professional life.

Read it your way

This book isn't meant to be read once and forgotten. Instead, think of it as a training manual, or a resource you can return to whenever you need to fine-tune your performance strategies. You can also jump into it at any point, based on your immediate needs.

For example:

- If you're struggling with burnout, start with Part I: The new paradigm. In chapter 1, I help you identify the hidden stressors that drain your energy and the outdated productivity myths holding you back. And in chapter 2, I introduce the Cognitive Athlete mindset as a model for sustainable excellence.

- If you want a proven system for high performance, go straight to Part II: The four phases of cognitive periodisation. These chapters outline how to align your workload with natural cognitive cycles.

- If you're ready to implement real change, jump to Part III: Living the Cognitive Athlete way. Here I provide practical strategies, real-world case studies and actionable steps to help you apply these principles to your daily life.

As you make your way through the book and start to work with your natural cognitive cycles, you'll no doubt notice some cross-over elements and overlapping ideas. Recovery, for example, is an important component within the Performance Phase, rather than being something to only focus on in the Recovery Phase. Incorporating mini cycles into larger cycles of performance and recovery is an important theme throughout this book.

Take action as you read

This book isn't just about theory; it's also about action. To get the most out of the following chapters, engage with the exercises, apply the techniques and track your progress as you implement changes.

Throughout the book, you'll find:

- reflection prompts to help you assess your current habits and identify areas for improvement

- step-by-step action points for building routines, improving focus and structuring recovery

- real-world case studies showing how professionals have applied these principles to achieve lasting success.

For additional tools and resources, visit www.thecognitiveathlete .com.au. Once there, you can download free worksheets, templates and planning guides to help you create your own Cognitive Athlete plan and apply periodisation to your daily routine. These resources make it easier to structure your work, track your energy levels and create sustainable high-performance habits.

Commit to the process

High performance isn't about short bursts of motivation; instead, it's about consistent, intentional improvement. If you implement even a few of the strategies in this book, you'll notice a shift in your focus, energy and resilience. If you take advantage of everything this book provides, you'll have a clear framework for managing your workload, maintaining mental clarity and avoiding burnout so you can perform at your best — not just for a few weeks, but also for the long haul.

Let's get started.

Part I
The new paradigm

Before we can explore how to achieve sustainable peak performance, we need to address the root cause of the issue: the current operating model that dominates modern workplaces. Many professionals, whether in leadership roles, high-stakes industries or entrepreneurial ventures, are caught in a relentless cycle of constant activity, unrealistic expectations and increasing demands. This cycle often leads to burnout, stress and diminished performance over time.

In the chapters in this part, I lay the foundation for why change is necessary, and help you understand the problem before diving into the solution. Without recognising the hidden costs of overwork and cognitive fatigue, you can't begin to implement strategies for sustainable high performance.

In chapter 1, I outline:

- why high achievers are more at risk of burnout and why working harder is often counterproductive

- how the modern workplace promotes inefficiency and mental fatigue, leading to diminished creativity and decision-making

- the science behind cognitive overload and how chronic stress affects memory, focus and emotional resilience

- why traditional productivity advice such as delegating and time-blocking often fails in high-pressure environments.

The goal is to shift your perspective from seeing burnout and exhaustion as 'just part of the job' to understanding them as barriers to long-term success.

However, the Cognitive Athlete approach is more than this. A Cognitive Athlete doesn't just work hard; they also work strategically, balancing intense focus with structured recovery, so they can sustain high performance without crashing. They understand that mental stamina, resilience and clarity aren't just natural traits; they're trainable skills.

At the core of this mindset shift is periodisation — a system used by elite athletes that cycles between high-intensity performance and deliberate recovery to maintain long-term excellence. In chapter 2, I introduce this method and how it can be applied to cognitive work, helping professionals like you achieve more without sacrificing health, happiness or fulfilment.

The journey begins with awareness. Once you see the problem clearly, you can begin taking the first steps toward becoming a Cognitive Athlete and transforming your approach to work, performance and recovery.

The later chapters in this book guide you through that transformation, helping you unlock greater energy, sharper focus and more sustainable success so you can thrive in your career, without burning out in the process.

CHAPTER 1

Why high performers are burning out and how to stop it

Sarah was the kind of leader everyone admired. As the head of risk and compliance for a global financial firm, she had built her career on relentless hard work, discipline and an ability to deliver under pressure. She was the definition of high performance — sharp, decisive and always in control.

Her schedule was nonstop. Similar to Dawn in the introduction, she often worked 18-hour days, crossing over time zones with European, Australian and North American colleagues. Even as exhaustion set in, she powered through late-night messages, report reviews and critical decision-making.

Sarah's work–life balance didn't exist. Weekends blurred into weekdays. Holidays weren't holidays and were instead just quieter workdays filled with 'just a quick Teams message' and last-minute compliance reports.

She convinced herself she could handle it. 'It's just the nature of the job', she told herself. She wore her work ethic as a badge of honour. She believed saying yes to everything made her indispensable. She was proud of how much she could handle. However, Sarah's nonstop work ethic came at a cost. She was trapped in an 'always-on' culture, saying yes to every request, attending back-to-back meetings and squeezing in urgent tasks late at night. She convinced herself that if she just worked a little harder, a little longer, she could stay on top of it all.

But that wasn't true.

Sarah had always been meticulous about preparing for meetings, and especially those with the global leadership team. As the head of risk and compliance, her end-of-year report was critical. It was her opportunity to:

- demonstrate how her team had protected the company from financial and reputational risk

- present key compliance trends and regulatory updates

- prove that risk management was aligned with the business strategy.

Normally, she would have spent hours fact-checking every number in her report, running through key insights with her team and anticipating tough questions. But this time, she hadn't even reviewed the report properly — because she was simply too busy.

Sarah had spent weeks juggling multiple high-priority projects, leading investigations and answering urgent requests from leadership — basically saying yes to everything. The meeting had snuck up on her not because she didn't care, but because she had been so overwhelmed. She simply hadn't had time to check in with her team and confirm the accuracy of the data.

Minutes before the meeting, she had just finished another Teams call — in this case, a tense performance management discussion with a struggling team member that demanded immediate attention. The conversation had been draining. She had gone in prepared to give constructive feedback, but had instead found herself caught in an emotional back-and-forth. The employee pushed back on her assessment, arguing that unrealistic workloads and competing priorities were to blame.

Deep down, she knew they weren't wrong.

By the time she ended the call, her mind was still racing and her stress levels were spiking. She had no time to reset before stepping into one of the most important meetings of the year. She logged into the leadership meeting feeling scattered, mentally drained and completely unprepared. Still, she put on her best professional face and began her presentation.

As she flipped through the slides, however, her usual confidence wasn't there. She stumbled over key points, second-guessing the numbers as she read them aloud.

Then came the questions. One of the senior executives asked her to explain a discrepancy in the compliance reporting figures. She froze as her mind went blank. She knew she should have the answer, but she didn't. She had skipped the usual pre-meeting briefing with her team and now, in front of the most senior leaders in the company, her lack of preparation was painfully obvious. She tried to recover, flipping through her notes and scanning the numbers, but she couldn't connect the dots fast enough.

Another leader asked a follow-up question in an area she could usually talk about effortlessly. But the words wouldn't come. The silence stretched. She could feel the tension in the meeting.

She glanced at the screen, scanning the faces of the executives. Some were looking down and taking notes; most looked unimpressed. Their expressions spoke volumes—doubt, concern and loss of confidence. Her credibility as a leader of risk and compliance had just taken a massive hit.

The meeting ended, but the embarrassment remained. She logged off the call and sat completely still at her desk. She had never dropped the ball like that before. She didn't need a call from the CEO to tell her how badly she had messed up, or an email from her boss to confirm what she already knew.

Her stomach twisted as she replayed the meeting in her head — reliving her silence and hesitation, the looks on the executives' faces. She had spent years building a reputation for excellence. After one bad meeting, it felt like it had all come crashing down.

The worst part was that she knew why it had happened. She wasn't failing because she wasn't capable. She was failing because she was exhausted. She had said yes to everything — every meeting, every request and every last-minute 'urgent' task. She had pushed through exhaustion for so long that she had stopped recognising the warning signs.

That night, as she lay awake at 1 am, scrolling through unread emails, an unsettling thought crossed her mind: *How much longer can I keep this up?*

Deep down, she already knew the answer.

The silent epidemic of modern professionals

No doubt you've noticed similar patterns within Dawn's story from the introduction and Sarah's story. These stories aren't unique. They're part of the silent epidemic that's attacking too many modern professionals — people across industries pushing themselves to the brink, mistaking constant busyness for real progress.

Technology has made it virtually impossible to switch off. Even after hours, the pings of new emails and vibrations of Teams messages or unread notifications create an unspoken expectation to always be available. Companies may not explicitly demand it, but the pressure to respond quickly, be 'on' and prove your commitment is ever-present.

Despite some government attempts to legislate against it, boundaries between work and life have all but disappeared.

If you've ever felt exhausted despite loving your work…

If you've ever felt like you're always behind, no matter how much you do…

If you've ever wondered, 'Is this just how work is now?'…

…Then this chapter is for you.

The modern workplace: A perfect burnout machine

Burnout isn't about working hard. It's about working without recovery.

The traditional work model was designed for the Industrial Age, where productivity was measured in hours worked, not mental performance. To understand this in more detail, and the issues that have arisen as production workers have evolved into knowledge workers, we need to start with one of the most transformative figures in modern industry: Henry Ford.

The creation of the production worker

In 1913, Ford revolutionised manufacturing by introducing the moving assembly line at his Highland Park plant in Michigan. While building a single Model T had previously taken a skilled team more than 12 hours, the job could now be completed in just 93 minutes.

This innovation wasn't just about machinery; it was about redefining the role of the worker. Ford's genius lay in breaking down the production process into a series of simple, repeatable tasks. Each worker was trained to perform one specific motion, again and again, as the car moved down the line.

By removing the need for individual craftsmanship or problem-solving, Ford massively increased efficiency, reducing training time and dependency on skilled labour. Workers became interchangeable parts in a greater system, cogs in a machine, and built for speed rather than creativity.

But this kind of work came at a cost. It was mind-numbing, repetitive and exhausting. Turnover at the plant was sky-high. In fact, Ford had to hire thousands more workers than he needed because so many would quit within weeks.

To combat this, he introduced a radical idea for the time: doubling wages to $5 a day. This move certainly shocked the business world, but it worked. Workers stayed, absenteeism dropped and productivity climbed. The Ford production model was hailed as a miracle of modern efficiency, and soon became the gold standard for 20th-century work design.

Its influence also extended far beyond the factory, with Ford's approach shaping how we think about work itself. The priorities for all kinds of production became to:

- standardise tasks

- maximise throughput

- track success by time and output

- reward endurance rather than insight.

This mindset has infiltrated office culture, schools and management theory. Even today, phrases such as 'clocking in', 'production targets', or 'efficiency metrics' are heard in environments that have nothing to do with producing a physical product.

What Ford built was designed for a different world — a world of physical labour, where success is measured in units per hour, not ideas per minute. The model was perfect for its time. Yet now, more than a century later, many of us are still working like we're on the assembly line, even though the work we do and the technology we use has completely changed. Professionals today are still expected to adhere to routines rooted in the industrial era — including fixed hours, rigid schedules and constant output.

Worse, our education systems still train our children for output over insight. These systems reward completion and compliance, rather than deep work or curiosity. Professionals enter the workforce already conditioned to prioritise doing over thinking, which only reinforces the burnout cycle.

The evolution of the knowledge worker

Knowledge work is fundamentally different from production work. While a factory worker might repeat the same sequence of physical tasks for eight hours, a professional worker today—such as a team leader, analyst or strategist—might bounce between a high-stakes client meeting, drafting a report, solving an urgent issue and managing people dynamics. This kind of day requires cognitive flexibility, creativity, decision-making and emotional regulation. Yet many workplaces treat both types of labour in the same way, valuing time-in-seat and availability over quality of thought.

Modern economies are now powered by ideas, innovation and problem-solving. Success today isn't measured by how many units you can produce in an hour, but by how effectively you think, how strategically you act and how creatively you innovate under pressure.

In short, we are no longer production workers but are 'knowledge workers'—a term coined by Peter Drucker in the 1950s to describe professionals who use intellect, analysis and decision-making as their core value drivers. In today's world, these are the people designing systems, developing strategy, interpreting data, writing code, advising clients, creating campaigns, and solving complex problems that machines or automation can't.

Unlike factory workers, who thrive in predictable, task-based environments, knowledge workers operate in ambiguity and complexity. They're expected to manage conflicting priorities, generate insights, collaborate across time zones and constantly adapt to change.

Yet, despite this seismic shift in how we work, many workplaces still treat knowledge workers as if they're on a factory floor.

They're expected to:

- power through hours of uninterrupted screen time, ignoring how cognitive performance naturally ebbs and flows

- jump from meeting to meeting, as if productivity is measured by how booked your calendar is

- respond instantly to a barrage of emails and messages, as though they were widgets on a conveyor belt.

This mindset, rooted in industrial-era productivity models, is breaking modern professionals. It assumes that the brain is a machine with infinite output, rather than a living system with limits, rhythms and needs for recovery. The result is exhausted employees with diminished focus and shallow thinking — and a culture where burnout is worn like a badge of honour rather than a red flag.

In the modern workplace, the vast majority of us are not building cars; we're building ideas, strategies, campaigns, code, content, models and experiences. And these don't come from repetition, but from clarity, creativity and deep work — and periods of downtime and recovery.

Studies show that the prefrontal cortex, responsible for decision-making, focus and creativity, fatigues after 90 to 120 minutes of intense work. Yet, most professionals work in four- to six-hour stretches, ignoring natural energy fluctuations.

Instead of structuring work around our cognitive strengths, we attempt to grind through exhaustion, resulting in slower thinking, poor decisions and increased stress.

Trying to apply Ford's factory model to today's knowledge economy is like asking a marathon runner to train on an assembly line. It's misaligned with the nature of the work and ultimately unsustainable.

Treating our brains like machines is leading to burnout

The human brain isn't wired for constant, uninterrupted work. Unlike computers, which can run at full capacity indefinitely, our cognitive performance operates in cycles. And while economies may have shifted for most developed countries, our approach to work hasn't evolved — in fact, in many ways, it's gotten worse.

With 24/7 connectivity, for example, we're never truly off. And this 'always-on' culture is destroying focus. Consider the following:

- The average American checks their phone 352 times a day (according to 2022 research from tech care company Asurion).

- Over 70 per cent of employees report frequent interruptions during their workdays (according to *Forbes* research from 2016).

- Microsoft research shows that people spend 57 per cent of their work time communicating and coordinating, leaving only 43 per cent for actual, meaningful work.

This creates a cycle of constant reactivity where deep, focused work is replaced by shallow, scattered attention. This can raise stress levels — and stress without recovery leads to burnout

Stress itself isn't inherently bad. In fact, short-term stress can enhance performance through triggering the fight-or-flight response, sharpening focus and boosting adrenaline.

The problem arises when stress becomes chronic, with no opportunity for deliberate recovery. Chronic stress has a number of knock-on effects:

- It elevates cortisol, which impairs memory, focus and emotional regulation.

- It contributes to sleep deprivation, which studies show can reduce the brain's ability to form new memories by up to 40 per cent (see, for example, research from Seung-Schik Yoo and colleagues from 2007), and impair judgement and decision-making, increasing risky choices (according to 2011 research from Vinod Venkatraman and colleagues).

- Ultimately, it results in burned-out employees, and these employees are 63 per cent more likely to take sick leave (according to a 2020 Gallup report).

What was once a temporary push turns into a permanent grind—and, eventually, mental and physical collapse.

The cost of ignoring burnout

Chris prided himself on being the one who could handle pressure. As a senior project manager on a government infrastructure project, he was used to long hours, shifting demands and tight deadlines.

His days started before sunrise. From 5 am, he was answering emails, reviewing reports and preparing for a gauntlet of meetings. Back-to-back calls with engineers, suppliers, contractors and executives filled every hour. His phone never stopped buzzing.

Lunch was an afterthought. He skipped breaks and stayed late, catching up on everything he couldn't do between meetings. The weight of each project sat squarely on his shoulders, and any delay could cost the company millions.

He felt constantly behind. He was mentally drained, overwhelmed by detail and struggling to keep pace with the chaos. But he kept pushing, convinced that hard work and endurance would get him through.

Until the day it didn't.

Amid the noise of a hundred moving parts, Chris signed off on a design change that he believed was necessary to avoid a delay. He didn't double-check with the engineering lead because there wasn't time. Based on earlier discussions, it seemed like a safe call—but it wasn't.

The design clashed with downstream specifications, resulting in major errors, production waste and delays. Tens of thousands of dollars were lost in rework and labour. Contractors had to be rescheduled. The entire project timeline slipped, triggering penalties and shaking client confidence.

Chris was stunned. He knew he wasn't careless. He was just exhausted. Weeks of cognitive overload had caught up to him. The mistake wasn't a reflection of his skill or intelligence, but a sign that his brain had hit its limit. This was the cost of nonstop output without recovery.

Chris's story is a warning. Even the most capable professionals can falter when they ignore their limits. Burnout doesn't show up as laziness; it shows up as errors, hesitation and costly decisions made under stress. And burnout isn't just about feeling tired; it's a full-body shutdown that affects cognition, emotions and physical health. Many high performers believe they can simply push through exhaustion, but the cost of ignoring burnout is far greater than most realise.

When left unchecked, burnout can not only harm individuals but also cripple entire teams, businesses and industries.

Cognitive decline: When your brain starts failing you

You know that feeling when your brain just won't work any more? You stare at an email, re-reading the same line over and over. The simple decision about what to write and how to respond suddenly feels impossible. That's cognitive fatigue in action.

Cognitive fatigue is so much more than a temporary inconvenience — it can also rewire the brain. Studies show that prolonged stress shrinks the prefrontal cortex, the part of the brain responsible for problem-solving, focus and decision-making. At the same time, it over-activates the amygdala, the part responsible for stress and emotional reactivity.

Interestingly, cognitive fatigue also kicks in after a certain period of deep focus. Your brain consumes about 20 per cent of your body's energy, even though it only makes up 2 per cent of your total body weight. It relies on glucose and oxygen to function properly, but when you engage in deep focus, the prefrontal cortex burns through those resources quickly.

Studies show that a decline in neural activity in the frontal lobe — either from stress or after a few hours of deep work — leads to:

- *Slower thinking:* Complex decisions that once felt easy now seem overwhelming. Tasks take longer and feel harder.

- *Increased errors:* Small mistakes creep in, affecting performance and credibility.

- *Reduced creativity and problem-solving ability:* Innovation and problem-solving decline, replaced by reactive thinking. Decisions that once felt clear now seem complicated.

In high-pressure industries such as finance and healthcare, cognitive overload has been directly linked to higher rates of costly mistakes, from miscalculations in billion-dollar deals to critical errors in surgery. (In relation to financial decisions, for example, see 2003 research from David Hirshleifer and Siew Hong Teah. Studies on cognitive load and surgery include 2023 research from Emma Howie and colleagues, and 2021 research from Nicholas Anton and colleagues.)

Even if you're not making life-or-death decisions, cognitive burnout means you're operating at a fraction of your true capability, which in turn means your work, leadership and career trajectory suffer.

I witnessed the effects of cognitive decline firsthand during my time in the military. As part of the training, we would run week-long exercises, deliberately depriving soldiers of sleep and mentally exhausting them to simulate the pressures of combat. As fatigue set in, their ability to think rationally collapsed. Simple speed-time-distance calculations — the kind they could normally do in seconds — became monumental challenges. They struggled to strategise effectively, with their once-sharp tactical thinking dulled by exhaustion.

One of the most telling moments was during night operations. A sentry, convinced he saw a figure moving toward camp, panicked and shouted 'Stand to!' (a command for everyone to get out of their sleeping bags and prepare for engagement). But there was no intruder. The Directing Staff (DS) were either at home or on rotation, and no scenario had been planned for an enemy attack at that moment. The soldier's exhausted brain had fabricated a threat.

In real combat, a mistake like this could mean soldiers end up killed or kidnapped by the enemy. But the lesson for all of us was clear: when the brain is pushed beyond its limits, reality distorts, decision-making crumbles and errors become inevitable.

This isn't just a military phenomenon; it's happening every day in high-pressure workplaces. Overworked professionals are misinterpreting information, making impulsive choices and losing their ability to think critically, often without realising it.

When you're exhausted, you don't just work slower. You start seeing problems that aren't there, missing the ones that are, and making decisions that have consequences.

Emotional drain: When you lose passion for work and life

One of the earliest warning signs of burnout is emotional disengagement. At first, this disengagement can be subtle — meetings feel more draining, motivation dips, and interactions with colleagues or family start feeling like just another task on the never-ending to-do list.

Over time, burnout leads to:

- *Detachment from work:* What once felt exciting now feels like a burden.

- *Irritability and cynicism:* Small frustrations trigger outsized emotional responses.

- *Strained relationships:* Family, friendships and team dynamics suffer.

This all affects how you turn up to work — or don't turn up. As mentioned earlier in this chapter, a Gallup report from 2020 highlighted that employees experiencing burnout are 63 per cent more likely to take sick days — and they're also 2.6 times more likely to leave their jobs.

Worse, burnout creates a ripple effect across organisations. Leaders who are burned out struggle to support their teams, and this leads to low morale, disengagement and increased turnover across the business.

Health risks: Burnout is a silent killer

As well as the mental effects of burnout, it's also physically destructive. Long-term burnout has been linked to:

- *Heart disease:* Prolonged stress raises cortisol levels, increasing the risk of heart attacks and strokes.

- *Anxiety and depression:* Burnout depletes neurotransmitters such as serotonin and dopamine, leading to mental health struggles.

- *Autoimmune disorders:* Chronic stress weakens the immune system, increasing vulnerability to illness.

The World Health Organization (WHO) recognises burnout as an occupational phenomenon caused by chronic stress that directly contributes to higher healthcare costs, absenteeism and reduced workplace productivity. Burnout is more than a personal problem; it's a public health crisis.

The business cost: Burnout is an organisational crisis

Companies don't just lose employees to burnout—they lose billions. According to Gallup research from 2022, stress-related absenteeism and disengagement cost businesses $322 billion annually in lost turnover and productivity.

Burnout leads to:

- *Higher turnover:* Replacing a skilled professional can cost up to 200 per cent of their salary.

- *Lower engagement:* Burned-out employees are less productive, less innovative and more likely to make mistakes.

- *Culture collapse:* A high-burnout culture leads to low morale, distrust and leadership failure.

In 2021, major companies such as Goldman Sachs and Google faced employee pushback due to extreme overwork. Junior bankers at Goldman Sachs, for example, reported working 100-hour weeks, leading to mental health breakdowns and resignations — and ultimately forcing leadership to introduce new workplace reforms.

So as well as being a personal and public health issue, burnout is also an economic and organisational crisis.

Recognising the warning signs of burnout

Burnout doesn't happen overnight. Instead, it builds gradually, creeping in until exhaustion, stress and overwhelm become the norm. Many professionals fail to recognise the warning signs because they convince themselves they're just 'having a bad week' or need to 'push through a busy period'.

But burnout is more than stress. As covered in the precious section, it's a state of chronic physical and emotional exhaustion that affects your performance, decision-making and wellbeing. If left unchecked, it can lead to long-term cognitive decline, health issues and career derailment.

So how do you spot burnout before it takes over?

Physical warning signs

Burnout often manifests physically before mentally, but many people ignore the signals their body is sending.

You should pay attention to any of the following:

- *Persistent fatigue:* Feeling exhausted no matter how much sleep you get.

- *Frequent headaches or muscle tension:* Particularly in the neck, shoulders and jaw.

- *Getting sick often:* Your immune system weakens, leading to constant colds, flu and other illnesses.

- *Changes in appetite or sleep patterns:* Struggling to fall asleep, waking up in the middle of the night, or relying on caffeine and sugar to get through the day.

- *Unexplained aches and pains:* Stress and exhaustion often cause physical discomfort that can't be traced to a specific injury.

Emotional and mental warning signs

As well as affecting the body, burnout also erodes mental resilience and diminishes emotional wellbeing.

Key signs include:

- *Irritability and frustration:* Small inconveniences trigger disproportionate emotional reactions.

- *Emotional numbness:* Feeling detached from work, relationships and even personal interests.

- *Loss of motivation:* Tasks that once felt exciting now feel like a chore.

- *Forgetfulness and brain fog:* Struggling to recall information, missing deadlines or losing track of priorities.

- *Increased self-doubt:* Feeling like you're not good enough despite past success.

Behavioural warning signs

Burnout changes the way you work and interact with others.

Look out for:

- *Working longer hours with less productivity:* Putting in more effort but getting less done.

- *Avoiding responsibilities:* Procrastinating, missing meetings or feeling overwhelmed by simple tasks.

- *Withdrawal from colleagues and loved ones:* Avoiding social interactions, skipping team check-ins or feeling isolated.

- *Increased reliance on coping mechanisms:* Using caffeine, sugar, alcohol or mindless scrolling to numb stress.

- *Ignoring personal needs:* Skipping meals, neglecting exercise or sacrificing hobbies for work.

Identifying burnout before it's too late

The following checklist can help you assess your current state, identify signs of burnout, and determine whether you need to make adjustments before it takes a lasting toll on your performance, health and wellbeing.

1. Check your energy levels daily.

   - Each morning, rate your energy on a scale of one to ten. Consistently being below five is a sign of chronic exhaustion.

   - Pay attention to afternoon crashes — are you relying on caffeine or sugar to push through?

2. Ask yourself: 'Am I just tired, or am I depleted?'

   - Tiredness improves with rest. Burnout doesn't.

   - If weekends or vacations don't restore your energy, you might be experiencing burnout.

3. Listen to what others are noticing.

   - Have colleagues or family members pointed out that you seem different?

   - Do people hesitate to interrupt you because they sense your frustration?

4. Track your work patterns.

   - Are you working longer hours but accomplishing less?

- Do you feel disengaged or cynical about work that used to excite you?

5. Take the Burnout Test.

If you answer 'yes' to three or more of the following questions, you may be on the edge of burnout:

- Do you feel mentally drained at the end of every workday?

- Do you find it hard to focus on tasks you once did easily?

- Do you struggle to switch off from work, even in your free time?

- Have you felt more impatient or emotionally detached recently?

- Are you neglecting personal wellbeing (such as exercise, hobbies and relationships)?

Head over to www.thecognitiveathlete.com.au/resources to download this checklist. Once you're there, you can also take the full Burnout Test and get personalised insights on your risk level.

Recognising burnout early is critical. Once you see the warning signs, you can start making small adjustments before burnout takes over your career, health and happiness.

And remember—burnout doesn't just harm individuals. It also damages teams, businesses and entire industries. But the good news is that burnout isn't inevitable, and you don't have to wait until burnout breaks you to make a change.

Small, strategic shifts in how you structure your work, manage stress and prioritise recovery can completely transform your performance and wellbeing.

In the next chapter, I introduce a smarter way to work—one that prioritises sustainable high performance, energy management and recovery, rather than endless overwork.

Key takeaways

The key takeaways for this chapter are as follows:

- Productivity today depends on thinking, not repetition.

- Most professionals are using a system designed for a different era, and it's breaking them.

- Burnout doesn't happen overnight. Instead, it builds gradually through overwork, exhaustion and lack of recovery.

- Technology has blurred work–life boundaries, making it harder than ever to switch off.

- Cognitive overload leads to mistakes, poor leadership and reduced creativity, ultimately harming individuals and businesses alike.

- Recognising early warning signs such as mental fog, disengagement and emotional exhaustion is crucial for preventing burnout.

Reflection and action: Know the signs of burnout

1. *Assess your burnout risk:* Take the Burnout Test available at www.thecognitiveathlete.com.au/resources to evaluate your energy levels, stress and workload.

2. *Check your work habits:* Are you working longer hours but achieving less?

3. *Recognise the warning signs:* Have you noticed increased fatigue, frustration or forgetfulness?

4. *Reflect on your boundaries:* Do you struggle to switch off from work in the evenings and on weekends?

5. *Start thinking about energy management:* What changes can you make to protect your mental clarity and performance?

CHAPTER 2

The Cognitive Athlete mindset: A model for sustainable excellence

The biggest myth about success is that burnout is the price you have to pay. It's not. And many professionals believe that working longer, pushing harder and always being available is the only way to stay ahead. But research and the experience of elite performers shows the opposite.

Sustainable success isn't about working more; it's about working smarter. The key is to manage energy and not just time.

Most people focus on time management, packing their schedules with back-to-back meetings, long workdays and endless to-do lists. But time is a fixed resource, while energy is renewable if managed correctly.

By applying cognitive periodisation, professionals can:

- *Work smarter, not harder:* Achieve peak performance without mental exhaustion.

- *Maintain long-term success:* Avoid the burnout–recovery–burnout cycle and sustain excellence over time.

- *Protect mental clarity, creativity and decision-making:* Stay sharp, focused and strategic even under pressure.

Small, strategic shifts in how you structure your work, manage stress and prioritise recovery can completely transform your performance and wellbeing.

It starts with a simple but powerful shift: rethinking how you work.

And that's where the Cognitive Athlete model comes in. This isn't just a productivity hack — it's a shift in how you view work, performance and success in the knowledge age.

The Cognitive Athlete: A smarter way to work

In the 1980s, Bill Gates made an unusual decision. Twice a year, he would completely disappear from Microsoft — no meetings, no emails and no urgent decisions. He called this his 'Think Week', and it comprised seven days of uninterrupted focus, during which he shut out distractions, read research papers and mapped the future of the company.

It wasn't a vacation but a structured mental recovery.

Gates understood something most professionals don't: true breakthroughs don't happen when you're drowning in meetings and emails. They happen when you create space for deep, deliberate thinking.

During this week, Gates wasn't just working harder; he was training like a Cognitive Athlete.

A new approach to high performance

To thrive in today's knowledge economy, professionals must transition from the production-line mindset (outlined in chapter 1) to the Cognitive Athlete approach.

Like elite performers, Cognitive Athletes balance periods of intense focus with deliberate recovery. They understand that cognitive stamina, decision-making and creativity require structured energy management.

Companies that also embrace this shift move beyond outdated productivity models and instead:

- prioritise deep work over shallow tasks, giving employees time for focused thinking

- encourage recovery, understanding that rest fuels innovation

- value impact over hours worked, measuring success by strategic contributions not just output.

This transition isn't just about improving individual performance. It's about creating workplaces where employees thrive, drive innovation and sustain long-term success.

The modern knowledge worker isn't a cog in a machine; they are thinkers, creators and problem-solvers. It's time to ditch the outdated production model and embrace a smarter, more sustainable way of working.

The science behind this approach

Cognitive Athletes train their brains like elite performers, ensuring they don't burn out their cognitive energy. And more and more research is now backing up why this approach is so powerful.

Your brain needs breaks

As introduced in chapter 1, after a few hours of deep work, neural activity in the frontal lobe declines. Decision-making and problem-solving get harder, and concentration fades — and you start looking for easier tasks. A study published in *The Journal of Neuroscience* from Grace Stewart and colleagues found that after prolonged cognitive effort, people default to easier, lower-effort tasks even when more difficult tasks would be more rewarding. This is why, after hours of meetings, you might find yourself procrastinating on easy admin work instead of tackling high-value projects.

Your brain works in cycles not straight lines

You wouldn't expect a runner to sprint flat-out for eight hours straight. Yet, most professionals assume they can stay in constant focus mode all day. But the brain doesn't operate in a straight line of productivity. Instead, it follows *ultradian rhythms*. I cover these rhythms in more detail in chapter 5; for now, it's important to understand that these are natural cycles that include peak focus periods that last about 90 minutes.

Research shows that:

- Peak focus lasts for about 90 minutes before cognitive energy naturally declines.

- After this period, stress hormones rise, creativity drops and mental clarity fades.

- Ignoring this rhythm and forcing yourself to work beyond these cycles leads to diminishing returns, reduced problem-solving ability and eventual burnout.

A landmark study from 1993 on elite performers, including violinists, athletes and chess masters, found that the best in the world didn't practice all day. Instead, they worked in structured 90-minute deep-work cycles, followed by deliberate recovery.

Cognitive Athletes structure their work in the same way, aligning their most important thinking tasks with their peak cognitive windows and taking breaks before fatigue sets in.

You make worse decisions later in the day

After a long day of back-to-back meetings, have you ever struggled to make even a simple decision such as what to eat for dinner? That's decision fatigue in action. Your brain has a limited capacity for high-quality decision-making each day. Every choice you make, big or small, drains mental energy.

As decision fatigue sets in, you become:

- more impulsive, making snap judgements instead of weighing options carefully

- more reactive, defaulting to easier, less effective choices

- more prone to errors as cognitive load increases and attention to detail decreases.

A 2011 study from Shai Danziger and colleagues found that judges grant parole more often in the morning but deny requests as the day progresses, simply because their cognitive energy is depleted.

Cognitive Athletes protect their decision-making power by front-loading their most important work when their cognitive energy is highest, typically in the morning, and saving low-effort tasks for later in the day.

Stress can boost performance—until it destroys it

Not all stress is bad—a tight deadline can sometimes boost focus, for example—but too much pressure can shut you down completely.

Psychologists Yerkes and Dodson discovered that performance follows an inverted-U curve, where:

- Low stress = low engagement (boredom, lack of motivation).

- Optimal stress = peak performance (high energy, deep focus).

- Excessive stress = performance decline (burnout, mental overload).

This relationship between stress and performance, known as the Yerkes–Dodson law, is also shown in the following figure (overleaf), along with the difference zones within this inverted-U curve.

Think of elite Special Forces operators. They don't train at maximum stress all the time. Instead, they alternate periods of high-intensity training with structured recovery to keep their teams mentally sharp and physically resilient.

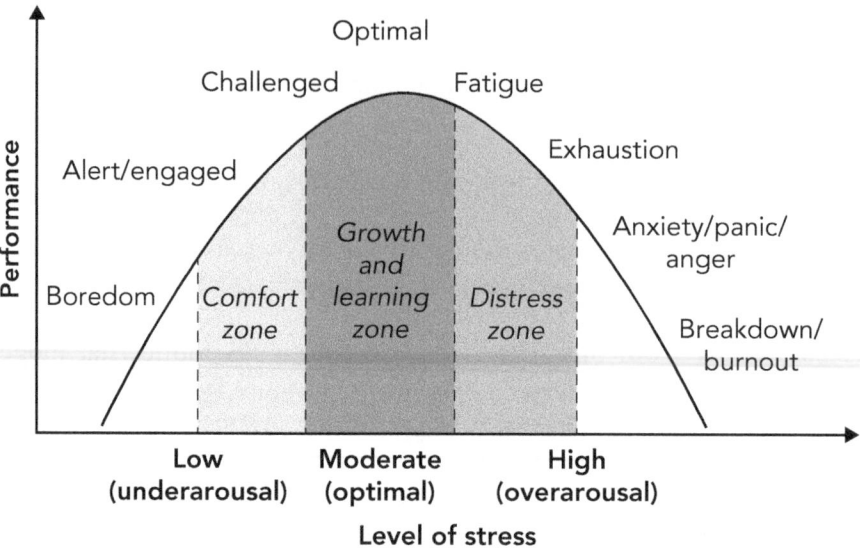

Yerkes–Dodson law: Inverted-U relationship between stress levels and performance

Cognitive Athletes train the same way, balancing periods of high-intensity work with strategic recovery, rather than operating at maximum stress all the time.

Burnout reshapes your brain (literally)

Burnout isn't just mental exhaustion; it also has serious long-term health consequences.

Long-term burnout has been linked to:

- higher rates of cardiovascular disease, depression and anxiety

- shrinkage of the prefrontal cortex (the brain's centre for decision-making)

- overactivation of the amygdala (the brain's stress centre), leading to increased anxiety and emotional reactivity.

Executives who chronically overwork face well-documented physiological and cognitive costs, including the following:

- elevated cortisol from sustained work stress

- reduced cognitive performance with long working hours

- weaker problem-solving and decision-making under stress and fatigue due to prefrontal cortex impairment.

Multiple studies into the effects of stress and overwork are included in the references at the end of this book.

Cognitive Athletes avoid burnout by respecting their body's natural limits and balancing focus with recovery, rather than ignoring mental fatigue until it's too late.

The solution: Work like a Cognitive Athlete

Most professionals treat work like a never-ending marathon, believing that pushing through exhaustion will lead to success. But the world's top performers — whether in sports, business or creative industries — don't train this way. They don't sprint through every session, ignore fatigue and hope for peak performance. Instead, they follow a structured system that balances effort and recovery, allowing them to perform at their highest level for longer.

Elite athletes don't train haphazardly. They follow a proven framework — one designed to build endurance, peak at the right time and recover strategically to prevent burnout. The same principle applies to mental performance. And this is where periodisation comes in.

Instead of grinding through nonstop work, top performers structure their efforts into cycles, balancing deep focus with recovery, and high-intensity execution with lower-intensity preparation. Periodisation isn't just about taking breaks; it's about working in rhythm with your brain and body's natural energy patterns, rather than constantly fighting against them.

Cognitive Athletes apply this approach to mental and emotional performance, ensuring that they're not just working hard, but also working effectively, sustainably and at their best when it counts.

They do this by:

- structuring their workload into intentional phases, aligning tasks with their natural energy rhythms

- using deep-work sessions strategically, rather than spreading their focus thin throughout the day

- balancing periods of peak performance with deliberate recovery, ensuring they sustain excellence over time

- training resilience rather than just endurance, so that stress is managed and performance remains consistent.

By shifting to this intentional approach to work, you'll achieve more, think more clearly, and sustain high performance without burnout.

This isn't about working less; it's about working better.

Understanding how a Cognitive Athlete works

A Cognitive Athlete follows a systematic approach to mental performance, just like a professional athlete follows a structured training program. Rather than basing their success on grinding harder, they base it on optimising cognitive energy, managing recovery and aligning work with natural performance rhythms.

A Cognitive Athlete is a high-performing professional who trains their mind with the same precision and strategy that an elite athlete trains their body. They understand that mental stamina, focus, decision-making and creativity require structured energy management, and not just sheer effort.

In elite sports, the best athletes don't train at maximum intensity every day. They follow a structured system of training, competition and recovery, allowing their bodies to adapt and grow stronger.

A Cognitive Athlete applies the same principle to mental and emotional performance. Instead of constantly pushing harder, they work in structured cycles, maximising their energy, focus and resilience.

For decades, professionals have believed that working longer and harder is the key to success. But the reality is starkly different: grinding through endless hours, skipping breaks and sacrificing sleep leads to mental fatigue, poor decision-making and burnout.

A Cognitive Athlete doesn't fall into that trap. Instead of treating work as an endless grind, they train their brain like an elite performer trains their body, structuring their days for maximum impact and long-term sustainability.

To help you fully understand the difference, the following table highlights how a traditional worker operates compared to a Cognitive Athlete.

The difference between a traditional worker and a Cognitive Athlete

Traditional worker	Cognitive Athlete
Works in a straight-line model of attempted full intensity every day	Works in structured cycles, alternating effort and recovery
Measures productivity by hours worked	Measures productivity by energy and impact
Ignores mental fatigue and stress	Recognises cognitive capacity and recovery needs
Suffers from burnout, exhaustion and disengagement	Maintains consistent, high performance over time

The following sections highlight how these Cognitive Athlete approaches can work in practice.

They work in cycles, not straight lines

Tim, a website designer, used to work straight through 10-hour days, struggling to maintain focus but thinking powering through was the only way to keep up. By mid-afternoon, he was exhausted, making more mistakes and taking twice as long to solve problems.

After adopting the Cognitive Athlete model, he switched to 90-minute deep-work sprints, followed by short recovery breaks. As a result he produced higher-quality code in less time and no longer felt mentally drained by midday.

They manage energy, not just time

David, a consultant, used to start his day with emails and meetings, leaving critical thinking for late afternoon when his energy was low. By 4 pm, his brain was foggy and even simple decisions felt overwhelming.

Now, he schedules his most complex tasks for the morning, when his brain is at its sharpest, and moves routine tasks such as emails to the afternoon. His productivity skyrocketed without him working extra hours.

They use recovery as a performance tool

Lisa, a marketing manager, used to power through lunch at her desk, thinking breaks were unproductive. By late afternoon, her creativity stalled and her decision-making suffered.

After learning about the Cognitive Athlete model, she started taking a 15-minute walk or doing breathing exercises at midday. Her afternoon energy levels quickly improved, and she made sharper creative decisions in the second half of the day.

They train focus and mental resilience

Before an important client presentation, Marcus, a sales consultant, used to stress-scroll his phone between meetings, feeling anxious and distracted. When he finally entered the room, his mind was scattered, making it harder for him to stay composed under pressure.

Now, he practices focused breathing exercises and single-tasking techniques before high-stakes moments. As a result, he enters meetings with more confidence, less anxiety and better presence, making a stronger impact.

Sustaining high performance over the long term

The world's top performers—whether in business, science or creative industries—don't just rely on talent or luck. They train their cognitive skills, protect their mental energy and structure their work with precision.

By adopting the Cognitive Athlete mindset, you can:

- increase productivity without working longer

- enhance creativity and problem-solving under pressure

- prevent burnout while maintaining high performance

- make sharper, more strategic decisions.

In short, a Cognitive Athlete is more than a hard worker; they are a high performer who optimises every aspect of their mental game.

Remember—the key to long-term success isn't endless effort; it's structured, intentional training of the mind. Cognitive Athletes don't waste time on low-value 'busyness'. They focus on high-impact work at the right time, in the right way. They don't just push through fatigue. They train, peak and recover strategically.

And the system they use to achieve this? Periodisation.

This structured approach to work allows professionals to maintain clarity, energy and focus over time, and avoid the burnout cycles that hold so many people back. This is the same performance framework used by elite athletes, performers and leaders to balance intensity with recovery and sustain excellence over time.

Becoming a Cognitive Athlete doesn't require extreme discipline, special tools or a dramatic lifestyle overhaul. It starts with reframing your relationship with effort, focus and rest.

To give you a better understanding on where you might currently sit in your relationship with these areas, head to www.thecognitiveathlete .com.au/resources to complete the Cognitive Athlete self-reflection questionnaire. This will help you rate how close you are to the Cognitive Athlete approach — or how close you are to burnout. You'll also be given a report with action points and strategies. You can keep your results in mind as you work through the following chapters.

In the next part, I outline the concept of periodisation, and the phases within this approach, in much more detail. Let's dive into how you can make this a reality in your daily life.

Key takeaways

This chapter's key takeaways:

- Like elite athletes, Cognitive Athletes train, recover and perform in structured cycles, managing energy instead of just time, using recovery as a performance tool and aligning their tasks with their natural rhythms to protect mental stamina.

- The goal for Cognitive Athletes is to work smarter and last longer at a high level.

- Energy management, not time management, is the key to sustainable performance.

- The Cognitive Athlete model balances intense effort with recovery to maintain clarity, creativity and focus.

Reflection and action: Your workday as a training session

Use the following table to reflect on your cognitive highs and lows during a typical day. This is your first step toward working like a Cognitive Athlete.

Your workday as a training session

Time of day	Energy level (high/ medium/ low)	Key tasks completed	Notes on focus/ fatigue
Morning (8–10 am)			
Midday (10 am–12 pm)			
Lunch (12–1 pm)			
Early afternoon (1–3 pm)			
Late afternoon (3–5 pm)			
Evening (5–7 pm)			

Part II
The four phases of cognitive periodisation

In chapter 1, we explored the challenges of modern work — including the always-on culture, the myth of working harder and pushing through, and the burnout cycle that so many professionals find themselves trapped in. In chapter 2, I introduced the solution: periodisation for the Cognitive Athlete. Now it's time to really dive into this concept and how you can apply it to your working life.

Borrowed from the world of elite sports, *periodisation* is a structured system that balances effort, recovery and peak performance, ensuring long-term success without burnout. Athletes don't train at maximum intensity every day; instead, they work in cycles, carefully structuring their preparation, execution and recovery to peak at the right time.

The same principle applies to cognitive performance.

Your brain, just like an elite athlete's body, needs deliberate training, maintenance and recovery to sustain high performance. Without this balance, mental fatigue sets in, focus diminishes and burnout takes over. Working strategically, rather than harder, is the answer.

The following figure outlines this practical framework for strategic cognitive performance, helping you periodise your mental workload and perform at your best when it matters most.

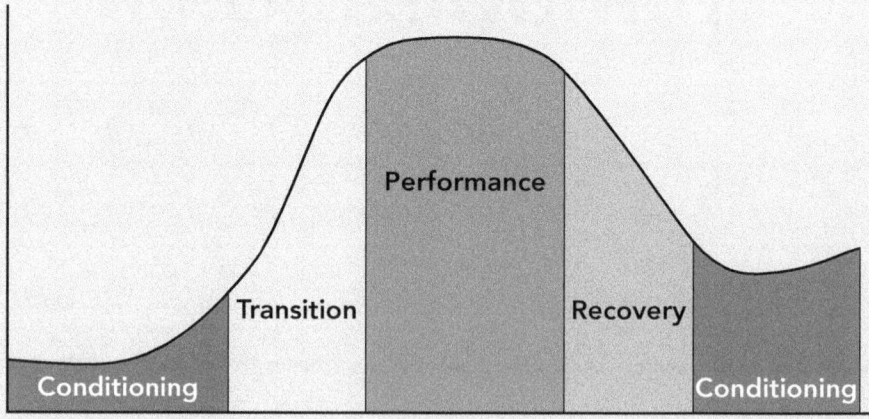

Cognitive periodisation

As shown in the figure, and just like an athlete structures their training, a Cognitive Athlete structures their cognitive workload through four key phases:

1. *Conditioning Phase:* Laying the foundation with strong routines, habits and resilience to prepare your mind for high-level demands.

2. *Transition Phase:* Shifting gears and priming your brain for periods of deep work, increasing intensity and refining focus.

3. *Performance Phase:* Operating at peak cognitive output, where focus, energy and creativity are maximised.

4. *Recovery Phase:* Deliberate decompression to recharge, maintain resilience and sustain high performance over time.

You might also notice that following this structure of cognitive periodisation means you don't start a new cycle at the same point as the last cycle. Working through the four key phases means you're better placed as you enter each new Conditioning Phase. Whether you're an executive, entrepreneur or creative professional, periodisation ensures that your mental energy is being spent wisely not wasted on exhaustion and inefficiency.

Each of the phases plays a crucial role in maintaining long-term cognitive stamina. As shown in the following figure (overleaf), the four phases also each consist of three important elements.

In the chapters in this part, I explore each of these phases, and the elements that support them, in detail. You'll learn how to integrate these phases into your daily, weekly and long-term work cycles, optimising when to push, when to pull back and when to recover so that you stay at your cognitive best.

By embracing periodisation, you can unlock better performance, deeper focus and greater resilience — all while avoiding burnout. You'll be able to work better and for longer.

Let's dive into the *how* of becoming a true Cognitive Athlete.

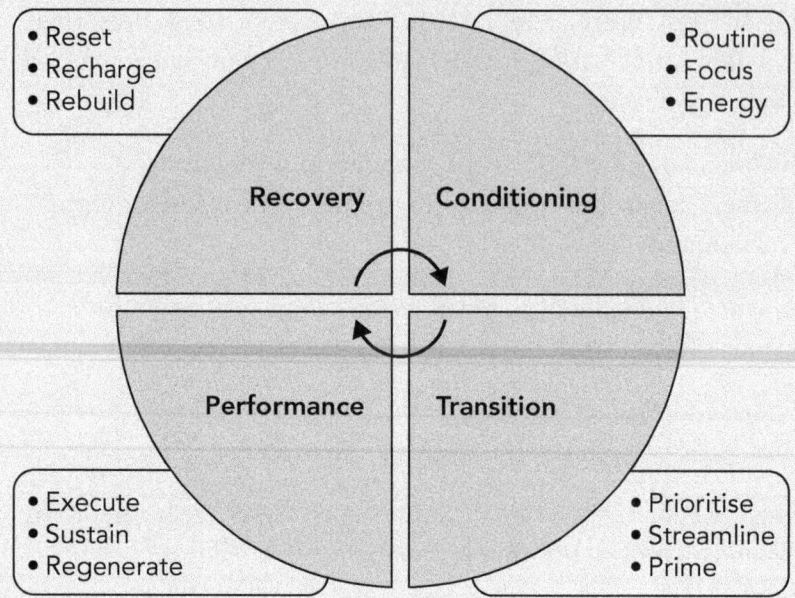

- Reset
- Recharge
- Rebuild

- Routine
- Focus
- Energy

Recovery **Conditioning**

Performance **Transition**

- Execute
- Sustain
- Regenerate

- Prioritise
- Streamline
- Prime

The four phases of cognitive periodisation

CHAPTER 3
Phase 1: Conditioning

Elite athletes don't step into competition without months of structured preparation. They train in cycles—conditioning first, refining their technique next, and only then pushing into high-intensity performance. Yet, in business and leadership, most people do the opposite: they go full-speed from day one, without ever conditioning themselves for the workload ahead.

This is why burnout is rampant, decision-making suffers and long-term success feels unsustainable.

Cognitive Athletes train differently. They build endurance, mental resilience and sustainable routines before pushing themselves into peak performance. The first step in this process is the Conditioning Phase, which builds your foundation.

Before I break down how to implement this phase, let's look at someone who learned this lesson the hard way.

Antonio's story: The CEO who had to step away

Perhaps you've heard of Antonio Horta-Osório, who for over 20 years spent his career climbing the corporate ladder. By the time he became CEO of Lloyds Banking Group in 2011, he stood at the peak of his achievements, tasked with steering the bank out of the global financial crisis. The pressure was enormous.

So, he did what high achievers often do: he pushed harder.

His days began before dawn and ended long after dark, packed with meetings, decisions and a relentless stream of emails. Weekends disappeared. Sleep became optional. He believed every minute spent resting was a minute lost.

At first, the adrenaline helped him power through. But soon, cracks began to show. His focus faded. Small decisions took longer. He became irritable and impatient. And then, the breaking point: five consecutive nights without sleep. His mind raced. His thoughts scrambled. His body began shutting down.

For the first time in his life, Horta-Osório couldn't function. So, he made a decision that shocked the corporate world: in November 2011, he took a leave of absence. A CEO stepping away from crisis leadership? Unheard of. But he knew that if he didn't stop, he wouldn't last as a CEO or as a person.

Taking time for reflection

Outside the chaos, Horta-Osório finally reflected. He realised his collapse wasn't due to a lack of effort. It was the result of pushing without preparing, and essentially running consecutive marathons without structured training. He didn't have a system in place to sustain high performance.

During his time away, Horta-Osório studied elite athletes, quickly realising that they didn't go full throttle year-round. They trained in structured cycles, balancing effort and recovery. That's when it clicked.

Horta-Osório realised:

- Rest wasn't weakness; it was fuel.

- Energy, not just time, needed to be managed.

- Elite performers don't just push harder; they also train smarter.

When Horta-Osório returned to Lloyds, he used these discoveries to redesign the way he worked. He made the following changes:

- *Prioritising recovery:* Deep, uninterrupted sleep became non-negotiable. As a result, his decision-making became sharper and his leadership presence stronger.

- *Time-blocking deep work:* Instead of drowning in meetings, he carved out focus periods for strategic thinking.

- *Embracing mental detachment:* He built in exercise, reflection and screen-free time to reset his cognitive function.

- *Setting boundaries:* No more reactive work at all hours. He created structured work–life separation, ensuring he operated at his peak when it mattered most.

The transformation: A new kind of leadership

With these changes, Horta-Osório came back as a clearer, calmer and more effective leader. He emerged as a successful executive and a respected example of modern leadership. Not only that, but Lloyds also returned to profitability. The company's culture shifted and employee wellbeing became a business priority.

Horta-Osório's story offers a critical lesson: burnout isn't random. It's what happens when you skip a vital phase of high performance, the Conditioning Phase.

Elite athletes never enter competition unprepared. They build stamina, routine and resilience before stepping onto the field. Knowledge workers must do the same, and train smarter rather than grinding harder.

So, ask yourself: are you conditioning for sustainable success or just hoping you don't burn out?

Understanding the Conditioning Phase

The Conditioning Phase is your mental training ground. This is where you build focus, resilience and endurance to sustain high performance without burnout, in a similar way to how elite athletes prepare before competition.

Elite athletes don't start with high-intensity competition; they start by conditioning their bodies. First, they train endurance and then refine technique. Only after this do they push into peak performance. You need to take the same approach for cognitive performance and knowledge work. Without structured conditioning to create a solid foundation of routines, energy management and mental resilience, poor performance and burnout is inevitable.

How athletes build a strong foundation

During my time working with professional football teams, I saw firsthand how critical the Conditioning Phase is to long-term success.

At the start of the season, players didn't dive straight into full-speed matches or high-stakes drills. Instead, the focus was on:

- *Baseline fitness:* Building endurance through high-volume, moderate-intensity training, such as interval running and strength-building exercises.

- *Technical repetition:* Mastering the fundamentals of passing, dribbling and shooting so they again became second nature under pressure.

- *Mental resilience:* Training focus, discipline and stress management to stay composed in high-pressure moments.

Every season, some players resisted. They wanted to jump ahead to high-intensity play. But by the time competition arrived, the athletes who embraced the Conditioning Phase performed with greater stamina, sharper decision-making and fewer injuries. The players and teams who skipped this phase, on the other hand, struggled to keep up.

Knowledge work is no different. If you jump into high-stakes leadership, strategy or creative work without first developing cognitive endurance, mental clarity and emotional resilience, you will hit a wall.

The Cognitive Athlete's Conditioning Phase

For Cognitive Athletes, conditioning is less about physical endurance and more about training the mind to handle sustained pressure without burnout. This phase helps build the fundamental habits, focus and emotional resilience needed to sustain peak performance over time.

The three key elements of the Cognitive Athlete's Conditioning Phase are:

1. *Routines:* Daily structures reduce decision fatigue and free up mental energy. Establishing a strong routine sets the tone for productivity.

2. *Focus:* The ability to concentrate for extended periods takes training, and can be enhanced through deep-work sessions, mindfulness and distraction management.

3. *Energy:* Instead of cramming work into every available hour, Cognitive Athletes align their workload with their natural rhythms and energy, working in high-focus blocks and recovering strategically.

The following figure highlights again the three elements that make up this phase, along with the three important processes within each element.

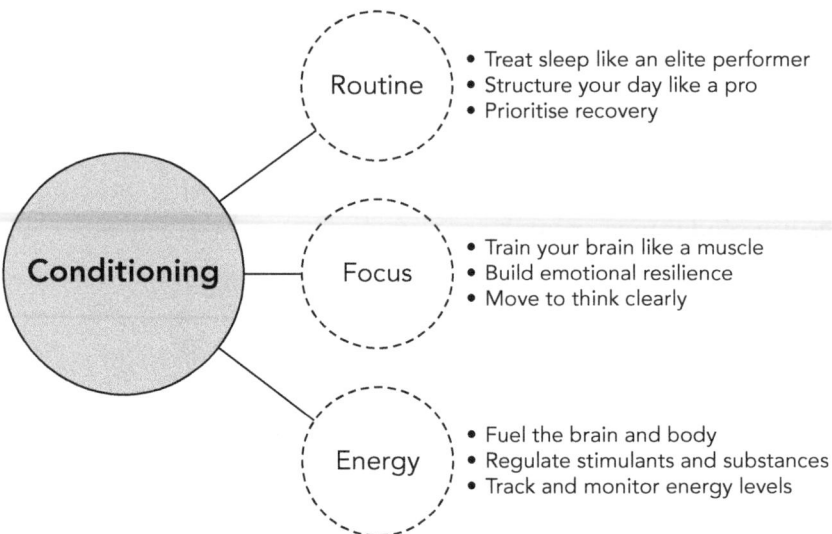

The three elements of the Conditioning Phase

Routine: Establish structures for peak performance

High performers don't leave productivity to chance. Instead, they design their days with precision, using structured routines to optimise energy, focus and resilience.

Without routine and structure, most professionals drift into reactive work: answering emails as they come in, sitting in draining meetings and constantly switching tasks. This leads to mental fatigue, decision overload and burnout.

Cognitive Athletes take a different path. They create routines that reduce decision fatigue, foster consistency and make peak performance habitual. When your day is built around high-impact routines, you remove unnecessary stress and free up capacity for deep thinking, creativity and problem-solving.

Structured routines can be broken down into three core components that help transform your productivity and wellbeing. As shown in the following figure, these core components are:

1. Treat sleep like an elite performer.

2. Structure your day like a pro.

3. Prioritise recovery.

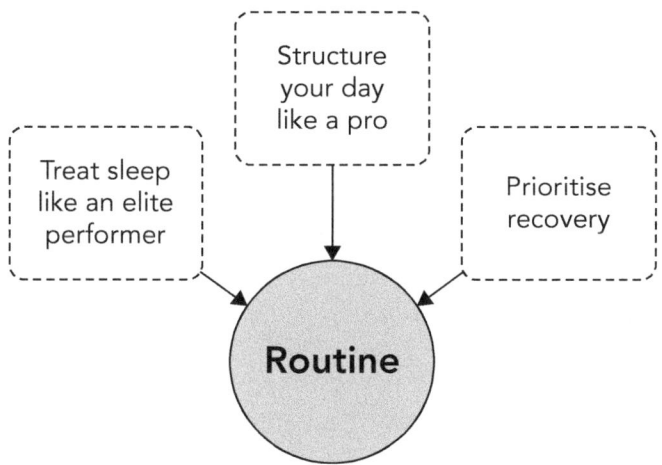

The three components of the routine element

Treat sleep like an elite performer

If you want to perform at your best, you have to start with your sleep. More than simply rest, sleep is a biological process that optimises brain function, consolidates memory and restores mental clarity.

Too many professionals sacrifice sleep for late-night work or early starts (or both). But the science is clear: even modest sleep loss impairs focus, weakens decision-making and increases emotional reactivity. Losing just 90 minutes of sleep, for example, can reduce alertness by nearly 33 per cent. Chronic sleep debt leads to brain fog, poor focus and emotional instability.

Elite athletes prioritise sleep because they know its impact. LeBron James and Roger Federer, for example, sleep 10 to 12 hours a night to maintain peak function.

When you prioritise sleep, your brain works better. Memory sharpens, reaction time improves and problem-solving becomes easier. You don't just rest; you reset for peak performance.

Here's how to optimise your sleep routine:

- *Set a consistent sleep schedule:* Going to bed and waking up at the same time (even on weekends) stabilises your circadian rhythm, improving energy and mental clarity.

- *Create a pre-sleep wind-down routine:* In the 60 minutes before bed, avoid screens, dim the lights, and engage in low-stimulation activities such as reading, stretching or journaling. Blue light exposure from screens suppresses melatonin, delaying sleep onset.

- *Optimise your sleep environment:* Keep your room dark, cool and quiet. Use blackout curtains, a white noise machine, or sleep masks to eliminate disruptions. Even minor light exposure can reduce sleep quality.

Structure your day like a pro

Your daily schedule dictates your energy, focus and overall effectiveness. Without structure, many professionals default to 'reactive mode', jumping between urgent tasks, fielding constant emails and putting out fires. This mode drains mental energy and limits meaningful progress. A well-designed routine, on the other hand, creates space for deep work, strategic thinking and recovery.

When you begin designing your day around focus and recovery, and not just availability, you unlock a new level of productivity. High performers don't just work hard. They work deliberately. That's the real difference between being busy and being brilliant.

Build a high-performance daily routine with the following:

- *Start your day with a morning ritual:* Instead of diving straight for your phone or into emails, start your day with intention. Begin with hydration, movement and setting your top three priorities. This primes your mind for performance and proactive work.

- *Block dedicated time for deep work:* Time-blocking is one of the most powerful tools in a Cognitive Athlete's toolkit. Instead of multitasking or reacting to every demand, schedule 90-minute focus sprints for high-impact tasks. Studies show that these uninterrupted sessions of deep-work cycles enhance creativity, problem-solving and memory. They also help your brain enter a 'flow state', where performance and engagement are at their peak.

- *Set clear boundaries for reactive work:* Don't let emails, meetings and admin consume your entire day. Instead, designate specific times for handling them to minimise distractions and protect your attention. This allows you to defend your deep-work blocks like you would any important appointment.

Prioritise recovery

Many professionals assume that working longer hours leads to greater productivity. But more time at your desk does not always mean better outcomes. In fact, the highest-performing individuals understand that recovery is not a luxury; it is a fundamental requirement for sustainable success.

Elite athletes never train at full intensity every day. They schedule recovery with the same discipline as training, knowing that without it, performance declines, injuries increase and progress stalls. The same principle applies to cognitive work. Your brain, like your body, requires structured rest to perform at its best.

Note that the fourth phase of the cognitive periodisation (covered in chapter 6) is focused completely on recovery. That phase is about taking a longer period of time to recharge and rebuild. Here, I'm talking about short periods of recovery taken through your day.

Here's how to recover like a Cognitive Athlete:

- *Take short, intentional breaks between focus sprints:* Every 90 minutes, step away for five to ten minutes. Research shows this can reset attention, reduce stress and improve overall focus. These breaks do not need to be complicated — walking, stretching or practising deep breathing all prevent cognitive fatigue and keep your mind sharp.

- *Implement an end-of-day closure routine:* Instead of working late into the night, wrap up your day by reviewing wins, planning tomorrow's priorities, physically shutting down your workspace and switching off work mode. This signals to your brain that it's time to transition from work to recovery.

- *Schedule intentional downtime:* Recovery also happens beyond the office. Engaging in hobbies, spending time in nature and pursuing non-work activities allows your brain to recharge and prevents chronic stress from accumulating. Some of your most valuable insights are also likely to emerge when you are not trying to force them.

When you begin treating recovery as a performance strategy, you create space for creativity, focus, and long-term stamina to thrive.

Reflection and action: Designing your high-performance routine

Self-check questions:

- Do I start my day intentionally, or do I go straight into reactive tasks such as email?
- Am I working in long, unbroken stretches, or do I take breaks to restore focus?
- Have I created clear boundaries between work and recovery time?

- How consistent is my sleep routine? Do I treat it as essential or optional?

- What non-work activities help me recharge—and am I doing them regularly?

Try this:

- Block one 90-minute deep-work session tomorrow. Protect it like a meeting.

- Set a wind-down alarm for one hour before bed tonight. Step away from screens and do something calming.

- Choose one end-of-day ritual to implement—review your wins, set tomorrow's priorities or shut your laptop with intention.

Focus: Enhance deep focus

Focus isn't something you either do or don't have; instead, it's a skill, or even a muscle, that can be trained and strengthened over time. Just like an elite athlete builds endurance to sustain peak physical performance, a Cognitive Athlete must develop cognitive endurance to sustain attention, process complex information and perform under pressure.

But in today's world, focus is constantly under siege. Our attention is fragmented by endless notifications, back-to-back meetings and the constant pull of digital distractions. This results in shallow work, scattered thinking and an inability to stay locked in on what truly moves the needle.

Here's the hard truth: if you don't actively train your focus, the modern world will train you to be distracted. And distraction is the enemy of deep work, high-level decision-making and peak performance.

So how do Cognitive Athletes fight back? They don't rely on willpower alone. Instead, they build focus through deliberate training, sharpening their cognitive endurance, strengthening their emotional resilience and even using movement as a tool for mental clarity.

Focus breaks down into three components, also shown in the following figure:

1. Train your brain like a muscle.

2. Develop emotional resilience.

3. Move to think clearly.

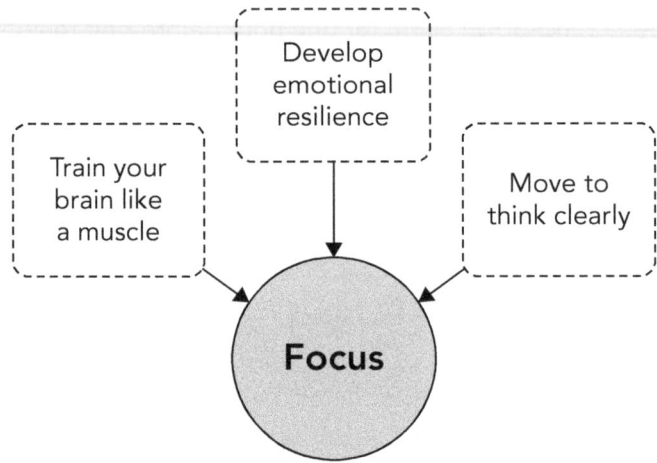

The three components of the focus element

Train your brain like a muscle

Let's face it—staying focused today is harder than ever. Constant notifications, task switching and the pressure to be always available leave many professionals feeling mentally scattered. The good news is that focus is a skill you can train.

Think of focus as being similar to a muscle. If you never use it intentionally, it weakens. If you overuse it without recovery, it burns out. But when trained consistently, it becomes stronger, more reliable and more resilient under pressure.

Cognitive Athletes know this. They do not wait for focus to magically appear when things get busy, but instead build it through consistent habits. This starts with one key insight: attention is a limited resource.

Each time you check your phone mid-task, let queries from colleagues interrupt you or bounce between projects, you spend that limited resource. Eventually, your attention runs low, leading to decision fatigue, procrastination and mental fog.

To keep your attention and focus in the right place, start to prioritise. Perhaps you've heard the theory that just 20 per cent of your tasks often drive 80 per cent of your results. I cover this in much more detail in the next chapter but, for now, try to think about which tasks drive your results and focus on those.

To build endurance, incorporate simple mental training strategies into your daily routine. Just ten minutes of mindfulness or breathwork can reduce distraction and improve focus. A simple practise is 4-7-8 breathing, where you breathe in for four counts, hold for seven counts and exhale for eight counts. Tracking what disrupts your attention — perhaps stress, external requests, emotional triggers or digital noise — also builds awareness and control.

When you start working with your brain instead of against it, everything changes. You become less reactive, make fewer mistakes and stay with challenging tasks longer. Your productivity improves — not through force, but through training.

Remember — if your attention feels scattered, it is not a willpower problem. Your focus is a muscle that needs consistent, intelligent training. Build it, and it becomes one of your greatest advantages.

Here's how:

- *Practice mindfulness or breathwork:* Just five to ten minutes of controlled breathing or meditation each day strengthens concentration and reduces stress. Meditation isn't about 'clearing your mind'; it's about training your ability to reel your thoughts back when they start to wander.

- *Reframe challenges instead of reacting negatively:* The way you interpret setbacks determines how they affect your focus.

Shifting from 'Why is this happening to me?' to 'What can I learn from this?' rewires your brain for resilience.

- *Track emotional triggers:* If you find yourself distracted or frustrated at specific times of the day, track these moments. Can you identify patterns? Certain people? Specific tasks? Awareness is the first step toward control.

Develop emotional resilience

As well as being focused, you also need to stay grounded — especially during high-pressure moments. Even the most structured day can unravel in the face of frustration, pressure or surprise challenges. During these challenges, emotional resilience becomes essential. It allows you to remain calm, clear-headed and effective, even when things go off course.

Think back to a time you felt overwhelmed. What was really going on? Often, the way stress disrupts your thinking is what breaks you, rather than the workload. When emotions spike, your brain shifts. The amygdala, a small, almond-shaped structure in the brain that handles fear and stress, takes over. Meanwhile, the prefrontal cortex, the part responsible for rational decision-making, gets dialled down. And so you react instead of respond.

Cognitive Athletes train for those moments. Rather than trying to eliminate stress, they learn to regulate it. This regulation builds a vital buffer between stimulus and response, allowing thoughtful choices rather than emotional outbursts.

You can build this buffer too. Tools such as deep breathing, journaling and reframing challenges into questions of control help reset your mindset. By reflecting on even small wins, you can train your brain to focus on progress, not just problems. This builds clarity and confidence under pressure.

Again, resilience is not about avoiding stress; it is about recovering faster, learning from setbacks and staying steady when it matters most. Like focus, it is not a fixed trait. It is a skill you can train. In demanding environments, this ability to stay composed is often what separates good performance from great leadership.

Here's how to build this skill:

- *Pause before reacting:* When stress spikes, take a deep breath before responding. This simple act can shift you from reaction to intentional action.

- *Use above-the-line thinking:* Instead of fixating on problems, train yourself to ask, 'What's within my control?' High performers focus on solutions, not obstacles.

- *Develop a daily gratitude or reflection habit:* Writing down three things that went well each day rewires your brain to focus on progress rather than setbacks.

Move to think clearly

If your brain feels foggy, your body might be sending a message. Physical movement and mental performance are deeply connected. In fact, movement is one of the most effective ways to clear your mind, sharpen focus and improve decision-making.

When you move—whether walking, stretching or exercising—you are not just benefiting your body. You are also increasing oxygen and nutrient flow to the brain, which fuels concentration and speeds up thinking. At the same time, movement reduces cortisol and boosts chemicals such as dopamine and serotonin. This creates the ideal environment for mental clarity and emotional balance.

That is why some of your best ideas happen when you're moving. Research shows walking can boost creative thinking by up to 60 per cent. Movement also helps unlock insight, problem-solving and perspective.

Cognitive Athletes use this strategically. They move before stress builds, not after. A quick walk between meetings, a few minutes of stretching after deep work, or outdoor training after a long day are all tools to reset focus and regulate the nervous system.

This is about more than fitness. It is about recognising movement as a tool for mental performance. Small, consistent bursts of activity, especially during the workday, can dramatically improve how you think, feel and lead.

So the next time you feel stuck or mentally drained, don't power through. Step away, move your body and let your brain catch up. Sometimes clarity is just a walk away.

Here's how to use movement to your advantage:

- *Incorporate micro-movements throughout the day:* Every 60 to 90 minutes, stand up, stretch or take a short walk. This resets attention and prevents cognitive fatigue.

- *Use standing or walking meetings:* Switch seated catch-ups to standing or walking meetings when possible. This boosts engagement, reduces stiffness and stimulates clearer thinking.

- *Alternate between sitting and standing:* Use a standing desk or makeshift riser to vary your posture. Aim to switch between sitting and standing every 30 to 60 minutes to reduce tension and maintain mental alertness.

- *Step outside for natural light and air:* Even a few minutes outdoors can boost your mood and focus. Try taking a break on a balcony, near a window or in a courtyard between meetings.

- *Schedule short movement breaks:* Block 10 to 15 minutes in your calendar each day for intentional movement, such as a brisk walk, a set of stairs or light stretching. Treat this like any other task on your to-do list.

Reflection and action: Enhancing your deep focus

Self-check questions:

- Do I have intentional focus habits (such as breathwork or time-blocking), or am I reactive to distractions?
- How do I usually react under pressure—calmly or reactively?
- How often do I sit for more than 90 minutes without moving?

Try this daily mini-routine:

- *Morning:* Ten minutes of breathwork or a short walk before opening your inbox.
- *Midday:* Take your lunch away from your screen. As a bonus, do it outside.
- *Afternoon:* Block 15 minutes for movement or reflection.
- *End of day:* Write down three things that went well, to help build mental resilience over time.

Energy: Optimise energy for cognitive stamina

Think about a high-performance Formula 1 car: sleek, engineered for precision and capable of extreme speed. But even with the best design and the most skilled driver, it's useless if filled with poor-quality fuel. It stalls, sputters or fails altogether under pressure.

Your body and brain are no different.

High performers are not only managing time but also energy. If you want to sustain focus, lead under pressure and avoid burnout, you need to fuel your system intentionally. That means eating to support brain function, managing stimulants such as caffeine and alcohol wisely, and aligning your daily rhythm with your natural peaks and dips in energy.

Cognitive Athletes understand that energy is their real competitive edge. By treating energy as a resource to monitor and optimise, rather than a battery to run flat every day, they gain consistency, clarity and control.

The three components of energy optimisation are:

1. Fuel the brain and body.

2. Regulate stimulants and substances.

3. Track and monitor energy levels.

These are also highlighted in the following figure.

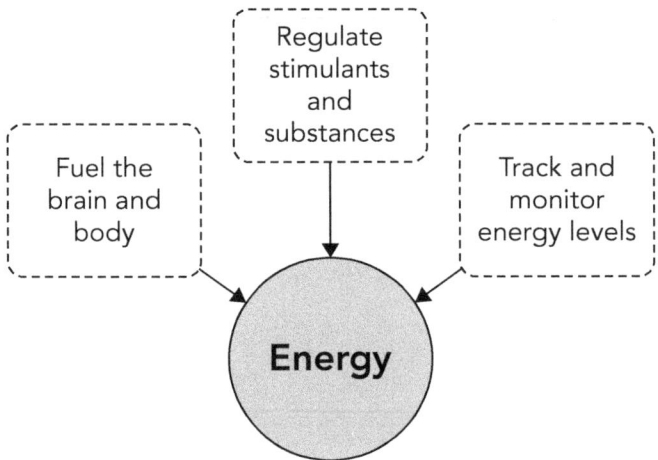

The three components of the energy element

Fuel the brain and body

When people think about food and performance, they often focus on physical energy—for example, how many calories they need to make it through the day. But for Cognitive Athletes, nutrition is also mental fuel, influencing far more than energy levels. Your nutrition also affects how you think, feel and perform under pressure.

As mentioned in chapter 1, your brain, while only 2 per cent of your body weight, consumes around 20 per cent of your daily energy. That means what you eat, and when, directly affects your ability to concentrate, make decisions and maintain mental stamina throughout the day.

Many professionals rely on quick fixes, such as processed snacks, sugary drinks or excess caffeine, to push through. While these can offer a short-term boost, they often backfire. Blood sugar spikes are followed by crashes, resulting in fatigue, brain fog, irritability and poor focus. Over time, this roller-coaster takes a toll on your resilience and performance.

Cognitive Athletes take a more strategic approach. They prioritise foods that support stable blood sugar, nourish the brain and promote gut health. These include lean proteins, whole grains, healthy fats and plenty of colourful vegetables. Together, they support mood regulation, memory and cognitive clarity.

Hydration also plays a key role. Even mild dehydration can impair short-term memory, reduce focus and increase stress. Many people start the day dehydrated, especially after coffee, and never catch up.

Fuelling your brain is not about being perfect. It is about being aware. When you treat food and water as performance tools, you unlock clearer thinking, steadier energy and stronger emotional control.

Use these strategies to fuel your brain and body like a high performer:

- *Prioritise nutrient-dense foods:* Opt for lean proteins, healthy fats and slow-digesting carbs such as oats, quinoa or sweet potato. These provide steady fuel and help avoid mental crashes.

- *Hydrate consistently:* Begin the day with a large glass of water and aim to drink two to three litres daily. Add electrolytes if needed, especially after intense physical or cognitive effort.

- *Avoid heavy, sugar-loaded meals:* These cause energy dips and impair concentration mid-afternoon.

Regulate stimulants and substances

Many high-performing professionals start their day with coffee and end it with alcohol to unwind. While this may feel normal, even helpful, daily reliance on stimulants and sedatives can quietly drain performance and recovery over time.

Caffeine stimulates the nervous system and temporarily boosts focus by increasing dopamine and cortisol. In moderation, it can enhance alertness. But excessive intake, especially late in the day, disrupts natural energy rhythms and interferes with sleep, particularly deep, restorative REM sleep.

Sleep disruption is where the cost becomes clear. Poor sleep affects memory, emotional regulation and recovery from cognitive load. That mid-afternoon slump is often less about workload and more about fatigue from overstimulation and insufficient rest.

Alcohol creates a similar issue. Though it may feel relaxing at first, it impairs sleep quality and reduces the brain's ability to repair itself overnight. Even one drink can interfere with brainwave activity, limiting recovery — especially during periods of high mental demand.

The Cognitive Athlete model promotes awareness and informed choices. Caffeine, used in moderation, can support focus but overuse reduces its benefits. Alcohol, a neurotoxin, can impair sleep and recovery even in small amounts. While some use it to unwind, frequent use disrupts cognitive function and resilience. Knowing these effects helps you make smarter choices for long-term performance.

Building awareness of when and why you rely on stimulants or sedatives helps you return to more natural energy regulation. Supporting your body's natural rhythms (covered in the next section) leads to more consistent energy, sharper focus and deeper resilience.

When you stop fighting your biology and start aligning with it, performance becomes smoother, steadier and more sustainable.

Here's how to regulate stimulants and substances:

- *Time your caffeine intake wisely:* Drinking coffee first thing in the morning spikes cortisol unnecessarily. Instead, wait 60 to 90 minutes after waking to allow natural energy levels to stabilise.

- *Limit caffeine after midday:* Caffeine has a half-life of six hours, meaning that afternoon coffee lingers in your system well into the evening, disrupting sleep and reducing recovery.

- *Replace alcohol with smarter alternatives:* Herbal teas, non-alcoholic adaptogens (natural substances that can help the body cope with stress), or simply better hydration help maintain mental clarity without impacting performance.

Track and monitor energy levels

Most professionals can recall moments of being 'in the zone'—times when they were energised, focused and performing at their best. But few know why this happened or how to replicate it—because they have never learned to track or understand their energy patterns.

Unlike time, which is linear, energy is cyclical. Your brain and body follow natural rhythms—circadian and ultradian—that influence when you feel alert, tired, creative or analytical. Ignoring these patterns is like working against the current. It wastes effort and drains performance.

As I've mentioned, many people push through fatigue, expecting to be 'on' all day. Cognitive Athletes take a different approach. They observe when their energy peaks and dips, and align tasks accordingly. They treat energy as data, tracking, analysing and using it.

You do not need fancy devices to start. A five-minute journal entry at the end of the day, noting when you felt focused, distracted or drained, can reveal valuable trends. These insights help you schedule deep work during high-energy periods and lighter tasks during natural lows.

Tracking also helps optimise inputs such as sleep, hydration and nutrition. If you crash every afternoon, you might be able to track this back to your lunch or poor sleep. If you note that a morning walk boosts your clarity, you know that is a habit to repeat.

Once you understand your energy profile and natural rhythm, you can stop guessing and start designing your day for flow. That is how Cognitive Athletes maintain consistent, high-level output.

Use the following strategies to track and monitor energy for peak performance:

- *Reflect on energy patterns:* Spend five minutes each evening noting when you felt most alert and when you struggled.

- *Use a performance tracker:* Track sleep, hydration and nutrition, making small adjustments to enhance energy stability.

- *Experiment with recovery strategies:* Test methods such as cold exposure, meditation or light therapy to see what enhances energy most effectively.

Reflection and action: Optimising your energy for cognitive stamina

Self-check questions:

- What did I eat before my last deep-work session? How did I feel 90 minutes in?

- How consistent is my hydration throughout the day? Do I start the day dehydrated?

- Am I using coffee for focus or to mask exhaustion?

- Do I notice any difference in sleep quality after alcohol, even after just one drink?

- When during the day do I feel most focused? When do I tend to struggle?

- Am I forcing myself to do difficult work during energy dips?

Try this mini energy optimisation routine:

- Morning:
  - Hydrate before caffeine (drink one glass of water as soon as you wake up).
  - Delay coffee by 60 to 90 minutes to support natural energy rhythms.
  - Eat protein and slow carbs for breakfast (for example, eggs and toast, or oats and yogurt).

- Mid-morning:
  - Schedule a deep-work block to tackle high-focus tasks.
- Midday:
  - Take a short walk or stretch after 90 minutes to reset focus.
  - Eat a light lunch with lean protein and veg to avoid crashes.
- Afternoon:
  - Have no caffeine after 2 pm, and instead switch to water or herbal tea.
  - Move between meetings—stand up, walk and reset attention.
- Evening:
  - Switch screens off 60 minutes before bed. Wind down with reading or light stretching.
  - Aim for a consistent bedtime—your brain thrives on rhythm.

Remember—you're not a machine. You're a dynamic system. Fuel, recovery and rhythm matter.

What's one small change you can make this week to better support your energy and protect your performance?

How Shavari used the Conditioning Phase to move from exhaustion to sustainable high performance

Shavari, the General Manager of Operations at a sports entertainment business, had built her career on hard work and relentless commitment. Overseeing multiple teams—including event planning, marketing, ticketing and venue operations—she was seen as the engine behind the company's success.

Her days were packed with meetings, operational issues and last-minute changes. Whether coordinating major sporting events or managing corporate pressure, the demands were constant. Shavari

(continued)

took pride in being the first to arrive and the last to leave. Long hours and an always-on mindset felt like the price of leadership.

But, eventually, the signs of burnout crept in.

She couldn't switch off. Evenings were filled with emails, last-minute approvals and nonstop notifications. Her phone was always within reach. Sleep became fragmented and unrefreshing. Exercise dropped off completely, and meals were quick, processed and often eaten at her desk.

Her edge started to dull. She grew short-tempered with her team, snapped over minor issues and struggled to focus in meetings. Small setbacks felt overwhelming. Despite working longer hours than ever, her productivity flatlined.

For the first time in her career, Shavari questioned whether she could sustain the pace. She knew burnout was looming but felt trapped in a cycle she didn't know how to break.

When Shavari and I sat down, it became clear she didn't need to work harder; she needed a new system. We focused on rebuilding her routine, focus and energy—the three pillars of the Conditioning Phase, which create the foundation for sustainable high performance.

Routine: Creating a structure that supports performance

Shavari's lack of structure meant she was constantly reactive, jumping from crisis to crisis. We reintroduced intentional routines to stabilise her workload and improve her decision-making:

- *Morning structure:* Instead of starting the day in reactive mode, Shavari prioritised her three most critical tasks before checking emails. This allowed her to stay proactive, rather than firefighting all day.

- *Work boundaries and evening wind-down:* Instead of working late into the night, Shavari implemented a shutdown process to mentally disengage from work. This prevented unfinished tasks from spilling into her personal life, improving both her recovery and family time.

- *Non-negotiable breaks:* We introduced a 60-minute midday reset, such as a walk, a workout or just stepping away from her desk. This helped Shavari maintain her mental clarity and prevented the afternoon crashes she had come to accept as normal.

Focus: *Reducing distractions and prioritising deep work*

Shavari's biggest challenge was that she was always available, which made deep work impossible. Constant interruptions drained her focus, forcing her into shallow, reactionary work. So we introduced the following:

- *Reducing interruptions:* Shavari relocated her office away from a high-traffic area in the venue. This reduced distractions, giving her uninterrupted time for deep work and strategic planning.

- *Prioritisation system:* We implemented a daily priority filter to ensure she focused on the 20 per cent of tasks that drove 80 per cent of her results. Before taking on a new request, she asked:

  - Does this align with my key priorities? If not, it's a no.

  - Is this my responsibility? If not, delegate it.

  - Will saying yes disrupt my deep work? If so, schedule it at a time that won't derail productivity.

- *Saying no to 'chancers':* Unplanned requests from colleagues trying to shift work onto her were a major distraction. Shavari learned to say no when tasks didn't align with her priorities, using her cognitive operating rhythm (COR) to integrate necessary requests without losing focus. (I cover COR in detail in chapter 5.)

Energy: *Rebuilding mental and physical stamina*

Shavari had been operating in survival mode, running on caffeine and adrenaline. To sustain high performance, we focused on rebuilding her energy reserves through the following:

- *Fuel and recovery:* She swapped processed snacks for nutrient-dense meals and cut caffeine after 2 pm to improve her sleep quality, ensuring better cognitive function the next day.

- *Exercise and movement:* Instead of skipping workouts, she committed to three 30-minute movement sessions per week, which helped regulate her energy levels and reduce stress.

(continued)

- *Active stress management:* Shavari introduced breathwork exercises (such as 4-7-8 breathing) and short nature walks to help reset her nervous system and stay composed under pressure.

The outcome: Sustainable high performance

Shavari's transformation helped her not only work less but also work smarter. She regained mental clarity, reconnected with her purpose and rediscovered energy for both her career and personal life.

Her team noticed. Her leadership presence improved. She was fully engaged in meetings, more approachable and sharper in her execution.

As a result, her department performed better than ever.

But the biggest shift? Shavari redefined success. She realised success for her wasn't about overworking or proving her dedication through exhaustion. It was about sustaining high performance in a way that was healthy, intentional and built for the long game.

CHAPTER 4
Phase 2: Transition

You've done the groundwork. You've built habits, sharpened routines and conditioned your mind for high performance. Now comes the pivotal shift from preparation to execution. This is the Transition Phase, and it's where even well-prepared professionals can falter.

Often misunderstood, the Transition Phase isn't just a lead-up to delivery. It's a performance phase in its own right. It's where you move from broad preparation to precise alignment — from generalist to specialist, and from readying to delivering.

This phase is also when pressure spikes. Stakes rise, time compresses and cognitive traps appear — including micromanagement, second-guessing, last-minute changes and reactive decisions. Without a strategy, this phase can unravel progress. For Cognitive Athletes, however, transition is where confidence sharpens, focus narrows and execution begins. It's about streamlining energy, priming the mind and zeroing in on what matters most. This is where preparation turns into performance.

Before jumping into each element, let's begin with a real-world example of someone who nearly broke under pressure, before reclaiming her edge.

Sheryl Sandberg's story: From overwhelm to IPO success

Sheryl Sandberg was no stranger to pressure. As Chief Operating Officer at Facebook, she had helped scale the company globally and turn it into an advertising powerhouse. However, according to her account in *Lean In: Women, Work, and the Will to Lead*, nothing tested her focus, resilience and leadership like Facebook's decision to go public in 2012.

The stakes were massive, including the following:

- a projected $100 billion valuation (one of the largest IPOs in history)

- intense investor scrutiny

- her leadership and legacy on the line.

Determined to deliver, Sheryl immersed herself in every detail, including financial models, risk plans, regulatory filings, investor materials and media messaging. From dawn to late at night, she was in constant execution mode.

As the IPO approached, the pressure became personal. Sheryl began second-guessing everything:

- Was the narrative strong enough?

- Were they downplaying risks too much or not enough?

- Could one misstep derail the entire offering?

Her instinct was to do more. She revised decks repeatedly, tweaked speeches last-minute and began micromanaging her team. Her communication became reactive. The more she tried to control, the more misaligned things became. Internally, tensions grew. Externally, investors sensed uncertainty and subtle shifts — the kind that mattered deeply in such a high-stakes moment.

Then Mark Zuckerberg stepped in. 'Sheryl', he said, 'stop trying to do everything. You've already built the foundation. Now, focus only on what moves the needle.'

It was a turning point.

Sheryl realised she had shifted from leadership to fear management, and was trying to control everything instead of trusting the ground-work. The Transition Phase demanded refinement, not overwork.

She pivoted immediately to the following:

- *Focused priorities:* She narrowed in on the top three investor concerns, aligning the team around a simplified, confident message.

- *Clear narrative:* Rather than overwhelming the market with data, she emphasised Facebook's long-term growth story, user engagement, global scale and ad potential.

- *Mental reset:* She worked with coaches to sharpen her delivery. They refined her tone, pacing, posture and ability to stay composed under pressure.

The transformation was more than tactical; it was also mental. With renewed clarity and control, Sheryl led the final stretch of the IPO with calm authority. Confidence returned across her team and the investor community.

The result? Facebook launched at a $104 billion valuation. Despite early stock fluctuations, the IPO was considered a success. While the company's scale and business model were key, insiders knew that Sheryl's shift during that critical window helped seal the outcome.

Reflecting on the experience, she said, 'Preparation is crucial, but execution requires clarity, control and the discipline to focus on what truly matters'.

In that moment, Sheryl didn't just help take Facebook public; she exemplified what it means to be a Cognitive Athlete in the Transition Phase.

Understanding the Transition Phase

The Transition Phase is the often-overlooked bridge between preparation and performance. During this period, all the foundational work skills, routines and habits built during the Conditioning Phase are refined, aligned and sharpened to meet the demands of a specific high-stakes moment.

In simple terms, you can think of this phase as the shift from general readiness to focused execution.

I've mentioned a few times that elite athletes don't train at full intensity year-round, and instead follow performance cycles. As competition approaches, they enter a deliberate transition. Training volume decreases. Precision increases. Their attention shifts from general fitness to event-specific performance. They rehearse technique, visualise success and simulate competition pressure to help ensure they arrive at the start line not just prepared, but also primed.

Cognitive Athletes—leaders, professionals, creatives and performers in high-demand roles—follow the same principle.

The Transition Phase enables them to:

- *Refine focus:* Narrowing down to high-impact priorities.
- *Manage cognitive load:* Clearing mental clutter and distractions.
- *Simulate pressure:* Practising responses under real-world stress.
- *Mentally rehearse:* Building emotional regulation and confidence.

When skipped or misunderstood, this phase can lead to reactive decision-making, last-minute overwork and burnout. High performers such as Sheryl Sandberg, who initially fell into micromanagement and self-doubt before Facebook's IPO, highlight what happens when the Transition Phase is ignored — and what's possible when it's reclaimed.

How athletes transition

As a Physical Training Instructor in the Royal Air Force (RAF), I worked with elite athletes as they moved through carefully structured Transition Phases. One of these groups of athletes was the RAF Ski Team. The RAF is a melting pot for high-performance sportspeople. Some are even full-time Olympic or national-level athletes, released from normal RAF duties to train and compete. Others develop through RAF-backed programs such as the Eagles scheme, the Snow Eagle scheme and the Alpine Championships — testing fitness, teamwork and resilience in demanding mountain environments. These experiences build not just skiing skills, but also the ability to perform under pressure, adapt to extreme conditions and bring that mental toughness back into service life.

Following months of conditioning, we shifted the team's focus to the demands of ski racing but concentrating on the following:

- *Lower body power and stability:* Training the legs, glutes and core to handle high-speed turns and rapid terrain changes.

- *Core and pelvic stabilisation:* Supporting balance and directional control.

- *Eccentric strength:* Conditioning muscles to absorb impact from landings and maintain form under stress.

But physical readiness alone wasn't enough. Athletes need mental clarity to compete at their best. This mental preparation — or transition training — was the final edge before competition. We incorporated three essential mental training techniques during this phase.

Breathwork for focus and nerve control

Ski racing requires split-second decision-making, and nerves can easily cause muscle tension, shallow breathing and reduced reaction speed.

We used the following box breathing technique (used by Navy SEALs and elite athletes) to regulate nerves:

- *Inhale for four seconds:* Fill the lungs slowly and deeply.

- *Hold for four seconds:* Absorb oxygen, keeping the core engaged.

- *Exhale for four seconds:* Release tension as lungs empty, keeping shoulders relaxed.

- *Hold for four seconds:* Maintain composure before repeating.

This simple yet powerful tool calmed their nervous system, lowered stress and sharpened focus, allowing them to perform with clarity instead of panic.

Visualisation of the course

Before each race, skiers visualised the entire course in vivid, first-person detail to gain precision in the mind before action. The athletes mentally mapped every gate, turn and movement, including the following:

- *Course reading:* Anticipating terrain changes.

- *Body positioning:* Feeling each lean and shift.

- *Environmental conditions:* Adjusting for light, snow or ice.

Studies show this kind of visualisation activates the same brain regions as actual movement, effectively giving athletes extra 'reps' before the race even begins.

Locking in pre-race rituals

Each skier developed a personal ritual or a mental cue to switch into peak performance mode. These included:

- clipping boots in a set sequence

- tapping ski poles together

- repeating short affirmations such as 'strong and smooth'.

These rituals weren't superstition; they were psychological anchors that created consistency, confidence and control under pressure.

The Cognitive Athlete's Transition Phase

An Olympic sprinter doesn't train at full intensity all year. As competition nears, their training becomes more focused. Volume drops, precision rises. They rehearse starts, visualise the race and fine-tune the details. Rather than doing more and preparing harder, they're aiming to execute better and prepare smarter.

This is the essence of the Transition Phase, and it applies just as much to Cognitive Athletes as it does to physical performers.

In leadership, strategy and creative work, preparation matters. But at a certain point, more preparation turns into diminishing returns. That point is the Transition Phase, when broad effort needs to shift to targeted execution. During this phase, you narrow your focus, refine your energy and get ready to deliver when it matters most.

This phase is where many professionals stumble. The pressure rises. Time compresses. And in an attempt to maintain control, people often overwork, micromanage, second-guess or make fear-based decisions. Instead of trusting their preparation, they default to panic mode — leading to scattered focus, poor decision-making and reduced performance.

Cognitive Athletes do it differently. They understand and manage cognitive load, or the total mental effort required to perform. Psychologist John Sweller breaks this into three parts:

1. *Intrinsic load:* The effort required by the task.

2. *Extraneous load:* Mental clutter from poor systems or distractions.

3. *Germane load:* Effort used for deep thinking, insight and problem-solving.

Cognitive Athletes reduce extraneous load during the Transition Phase by streamlining their environment, automating routines and simplifying choices. This protects energy for germane load, where high-value work happens.

They also minimise decision fatigue. Research by professor of psychology Roy Baumeister and *New York Times* journalist John Tierney shows that frequent decision-making reduces willpower and increases impulsivity. That's why high performers such as Steve Jobs wore the same outfit daily and why the military standardises gear — removing as many decisions as possible helps preserve cognitive energy for what matters most.

In practice, this might look like rehearsing a presentation, blocking in 90 minutes for deep work or visualising a key negotiation. These actions help simplify the unnecessary to strengthen the essential.

The Transition Phase is not a passive pause; it's a strategic pivot. It's the bridge between preparation and performance, and between being ready and delivering results.

Get this phase right, and you create calm under pressure, clarity in complexity and consistency in execution.

The three key elements of the Cognitive Athlete's Transition Phase are:

1. *Prioritise:* High performers succeed by focusing on high-impact work and concentrating on what truly moves the needle. This phase is about cutting low-value tasks and doubling down on deep execution.

2. *Streamline:* Peak performance depends on eliminating friction and reducing cognitive load. Streamlining systems, simplifying decisions and managing energy clears the way for focused, high-stakes work.

3. *Prime:* Top performers don't wing it. They mentally prepare for high-stakes moments, and use routines, visualisation and mental rehearsal to step into pressure moments with confidence and control.

The following figure highlights the three elements that make up this phase, along with the three important processes within each element.

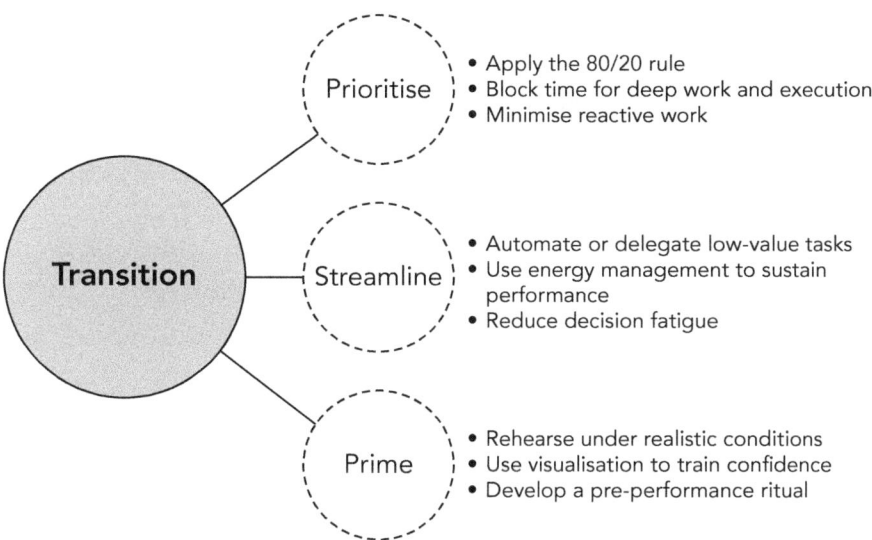

Three elements of the Transition Phase

Prioritise: Focus on high-impact work

Most professionals assume that being productive means doing more — ticking off endless tasks, responding to every email and attending every meeting. But the highest performers don't focus on doing more; they focus on doing what matters most.

In the Transition Phase, Cognitive Athletes work with precision to refine their priorities, eliminate distractions and channel their energy into the tasks that drive the greatest results.

This phase is about intentional prioritisation and choosing what truly matters over what simply demands attention. Without this discipline, professionals fall into the trap of reactive work, spending their days responding to low-impact tasks rather than making strategic progress.

Cognitive Athletes don't allow their workload to dictate their focus. Instead, they take control, identifying what is essential and eliminating, automating or delegating the rest.

The three core components of prioritising your work are:

1. Apply the 80/20 rule to your workload.

2. Block time for deep work and execution.

3. Minimise reactive work.

These components are also shown in the following figure.

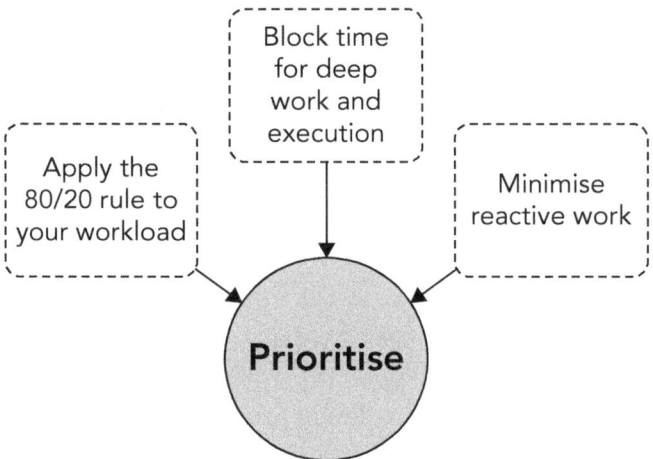

The three components of the prioritise element

Apply the 80/20 rule to your workload

The Pareto principle, or 80/20 rule, suggests that 80 per cent of your results come from just 20 per cent of your efforts. In other words, a small portion of what you do each day truly drives impact. The rest is often low-value activity that creates the illusion of progress.

Many professionals fall into the trap of staying busy, responding to every email, attending every meeting and filling their day with admin work. But high performers, especially Cognitive Athletes, work differently. They identify the 'vital few' tasks that produce outsized results and eliminate, automate or delegate the rest.

To apply the 80/20 rule, start each day by asking, 'If I could only work for two hours today, what would I focus on?'

This simple question forces clarity and helps uncover high-leverage actions, such as preparing for a key meeting, solving a strategic problem or producing work that drives long-term growth.

Once you've identified such tasks, protect them. Block out distractions and avoid shallow work. Use your peak energy to execute your priority tasks with focus and precision.

The 80/20 rule is not about doing less for the sake of ease; it is about focusing on what truly matters. Cognitive Athletes know that success does not come from doing everything. It comes from doing the right things exceptionally well.

Here's how to prioritise high-impact work:

- *List and filter:* Sit down and write out your full to-do list. Get everything out of your head and onto paper. Then, identify the top 20 per cent — that is, the handful of tasks that will drive the biggest impact.

- *Estimate time:* Estimate how long each key task should take — and try to stick to it. Remember Parkinson's Law here: work expands to fill the time available. Set clear, focused time frames to avoid overthinking and stay on track.

- *Schedule with intention:* Block time for these tasks during your peak energy hours. Treat them like important meetings. When you've blocked out time in your calendar, you're more likely to follow through with focus and discipline. (More on this in the next component.)

Block time for deep work and execution

Cognitive energy is limited. Like physical stamina, it declines as the day goes on. Every meeting, message and small decision drains focus. High performers protect their sharpest hours for meaningful work to ensure this is when deep work happens.

Deep work, as described by professor of computer science Cal Newport, is focused, distraction-free time for high-value tasks—including creative thinking, strategic planning and complex problem-solving. This work is not checking emails or sitting in status updates; it is dedicated execution that moves important work forward.

People who consistently prioritise deep work deliver clearer, faster and more impactful results. They stay ahead not by doing more, but by focusing better.

Like many, I used to try to 'squeeze in' key tasks between meetings. This ultimately resulted in distraction, under-preparation and mental fatigue. I learned that deep work must be scheduled, not squeezed. Design your day around it.

Cognitive Athletes plan deep work during their cognitive prime, typically mid-morning or early afternoon. A practical tool is the 90-minute focus block, which aligns with the brain's natural rhythm and balances intensity with sustainability.

During these blocks:

- silence notifications

- shut down your inbox

- use a distraction-free space

- let others know you're in focus mode.

Protect this time as you would any critical meeting. Research shows task-switching can reduce productivity by up to 40 per cent. Deep work, on the other hand, compounds over time, training your brain to focus faster and stay there longer. This increased focus results in higher-quality output, lower stress and a rhythm of performance built on intent not reactivity.

Use the following techniques to block time for deep work and protect your cognitive prime time:

- *Identify your deep work window:* Pinpoint the time of day when your focus is strongest.

- *Schedule 90-minute deep work blocks:* Reserve time in your calendar for strategic, creative or complex work during your deep work windows.

- *Set a 'no-interruptions' rule:* Turn off notifications, close your inbox and communicate your focus time to your team.

Minimise reactive work

Many professionals underestimate how much energy is consumed by reactive work such as replying to emails, attending unclear meetings and handling admin requests on the fly. These tasks seem minor but fragment focus and drain mental bandwidth. The real cost comes from not only the time spent, but also the constant context switching.

Cognitive Athletes protect their attention. They do not let emails or meetings dictate their day, and instead create structure around reactive tasks to stay in control.

Start by batching similar tasks into focused blocks:

- Check email at set times (for example, 11 am and 4 pm) instead of constantly.

- Return calls and handle admin tasks in grouped sessions.

- Block time specifically for low-focus work, rather than letting it interrupt deep tasks.

Next, challenge every meeting: Is it essential? Could it be handled through an email, shared doc or voice message?

The 'two-minute rule' can also help. If something takes under two minutes, such as confirming a time or sending a quick reply, do it immediately. If it takes longer, schedule it rather than letting it hijack your attention.

Also consider creating a 'reactive work zone' — a block of time near the end of your day for emails, admin and quick-fire requests. This keeps the middle of your day clear for higher-value work.

Minimising reactive work is not about avoiding communication, but about protecting your focus. When you take control of when and how you respond, you create space for clarity, execution and deeper thinking.

Here's a summary of how you can minimise reactive work:

- *Batch emails, calls and meetings into dedicated time slots*: Respond in those time slots instead of reacting all day.

- *Challenge every meeting invitation*: Is it necessary? Could it be an email?

- *Use the 'two-minute rule'*: If something will take less than two minutes, handle it immediately; otherwise, schedule it.

- *Create a 'reactive work zone'*: Allocate a set time to process admin and messages without disrupting focus time.

Reflection and action: Sharpening your priorities

Self-check questions:

- Am I clear on which tasks create the most value in my role?
- Do I protect time each day for deep, focused work?
- How much of my day is spent reacting versus creating?
- Do I control my calendar, or does it control me?

Try this:

- Ask yourself: If I only had two hours to work today, what would I focus on? Then do that first.

- Block a 90-minute deep-work session tomorrow during your peak energy window.

- Challenge the next meeting invite you receive. Do you really need to attend or could this be resolved another way?

Intentional prioritisation isn't about perfection; it's about focus, discipline and designing your day to deliver meaningful results.

Streamline: Reduce Cognitive Load

Productivity is not about doing more but about doing what matters with less friction. Many professionals confuse busyness with effectiveness, filling calendars, replying to every ping and constantly switching tasks. This drains mental energy and reduces performance.

As already mentioned, your brain has limited capacity for focus and decision-making. The more clutter you allow — from low-value tasks to constant interruptions — the faster your cognitive resources deplete.

Cognitive Athletes take a different path. They eliminate noise, delegate low-impact work and build simple, repeatable systems to preserve focus. Instead of trying to power through, they streamline.

They also manage energy, not just time. By aligning work with their natural cognitive peaks and reducing trivial choices, they protect their brainpower for what truly matters.

Streamlining is not only efficient but also essential for clarity, precision and sustainable high performance.

As also shown in the following figure, the three components of streamlining are:

1. Automate or delegate low-value tasks.

2. Use energy management to sustain performance.

3. Reduce decision fatigue.

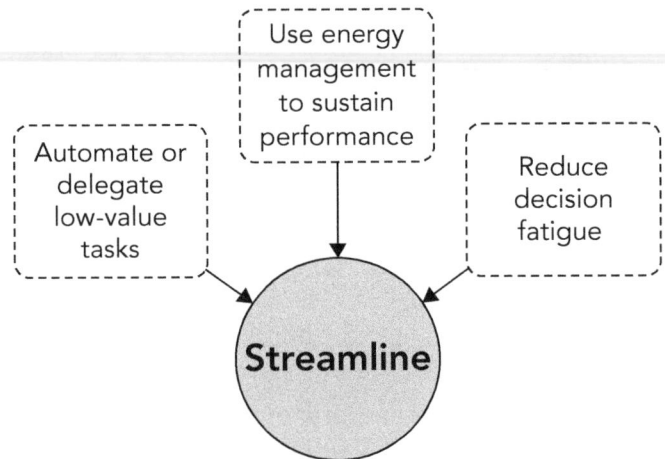

The three components of the streamline element

Automate or delegate low-value tasks

The brain is a high-performance engine, but it is not designed to manage an endless stream of small decisions. Every time you answer an email, approve a calendar invite or chase a routine request, you draw on the same cognitive resources needed for deep thinking and strategic work. As Daniel Kahneman explains in *Thinking, Fast and Slow*, mental energy is finite and every decision has a cost.

Cognitive Athletes protect that energy. They automate, delegate or eliminate low-value tasks to preserve focus for what truly matters. This is not laziness; it is performance strategy.

Automation is the first filter. Use scheduling tools, templates, email rules and task apps to handle repetitive actions. These tools guard your brain from distraction.

Delegation is next. Many leaders default to the 'It's quicker if I do it' approach, but that mindset steals time from high-impact work. If someone can do it 80 per cent as well, delegate it. Your value lies in where your impact is greatest.

Elimination is the final option here, and a quiet superpower. Ask yourself: Does this task move me closer to my goal? If not, let it go. Not everything needs to be done.

In practice, Cognitive Athletes regularly review their workload and ask:

- Can this be automated?

- Can this be handed off?

- Can this be removed altogether?

By building systems around these questions, they create more mental space for what matters most and they execute with more clarity, energy and intent.

Use the following strategies to automate and delegate:

- *Audit your week:* List all your recurring tasks.

- *Sort using the three filters:* Consider each task and whether could it be automated, delegated or eliminated.

- *Systemise:* Create templates, set up automations and delegate recurring tasks to free up time.

- *Schedule regular reviews:* Revisit your task list weekly to keep your focus sharp and your energy clear.

Use energy management to sustain performance

Time might be finite but it's not your most limited resource. Energy is. You can have an entire day blocked out for important work, but if your mental energy is depleted, even simple tasks feel overwhelming. This is why many people work long hours yet achieve little of real value.

As Tony Schwartz and Catherine McCarthy explain in their work on sustainable performance, productivity is less about time on task and more about the quality of energy you bring to that task.

Cognitive Athletes manage not only the clock but also themselves. They recognise that the brain doesn't operate at a constant level all day. Instead, mental energy fluctuates in cycles. As I've already touched on, peak focus, creativity and decision-making typically occur in 90-minute waves, followed by natural dips in performance. Trying to push through those dips leads to fatigue, mistakes and frustration.

Instead of fighting their biology, high performers work with it. They align their most demanding tasks with their cognitive peaks and schedule recovery during low-energy periods. Interestingly, while most people hit their stride in the morning, my peak energy consistently hits between 3 and 5 pm. That's when I do my best deep work, and so it was often when I wrote this book. The key is to know your rhythm and protect it.

Here's how to manage your energy more intentionally:

- *Work in alignment with your natural energy peaks:* Most people experience peak focus in the morning. Whatever your peak time is, protect it for deep, important work.

- *Take strategic breaks to reset focus:* Instead of powering through fatigue, use five- to ten-minute breaks every 90 minutes to refresh the brain.

- *Use active recovery, not passive distractions:* Instead of checking social media during your break, take a short walk or do a breathing exercise to reset mental clarity.

Reduce decision fatigue

Decision fatigue is real. After a long day of meetings, deadlines and constant problem-solving, even simple choices—such as what to eat, where to start and how to reply to an email—can feel mentally exhausting. That sense of being overwhelmed is not a lack of motivation; it's your brain signalling depletion.

Research by Roy Baumeister and colleagues shows that the more decisions we make, the more our cognitive control and focus decline. As decision load increases, mental resources run dry, leading to impulsive reactions, procrastination and burnout.

Cognitive Athletes recognise this and take proactive steps to protect their mental energy. Their goal is to conserve willpower for high-value decisions, not burn it on trivial ones.

In short: making fewer low-value choices equals more mental space. Streamlining decisions leads to better focus, stronger execution and higher performance where it matters most.

How's how to do it:

- *Create routines that remove low-impact or unnecessary choices:* Having a pre-set morning ritual, pre-planned meal options, a structured workflow or a predictable end-of-day routine reduces the decision load and simplifies the daily flow.

- *Batch similar decisions together:* Instead of deciding things one at a time, group similar tasks and make multiple decisions at once. Pre-scheduled meetings, weekly meal plans and standard email templates reduce day-to-day cognitive drag.

- *Use a 'default option' for repeated choices:* Having go-to responses for routine questions or standard processes for starting meetings, handling work, replying to requests or prioritising tasks eliminates hesitation and keeps mental bandwidth available for more complex thinking.

This approach is not about being robotic; it's about being strategic. The fewer unnecessary decisions you make, the more energy you'll have for critical thinking, creativity and leadership.

Reflection and action: Streamline your workflow

Self-check questions:

- Am I spending valuable energy on tasks someone else or a system could handle?

- Do I know when my cognitive energy peaks, and do I protect that time?

- Have I built routines that minimise daily decisions, or am I constantly choosing on the fly?

Try this:

- Identify one recurring low-value task this week you can delegate or automate.

- Track your energy levels across three days to find your peak productivity window.

- Choose one area to simplify—perhaps your morning routine, email process or meeting schedule—and create a default system to reduce daily decision load.

Remember—streamlining isn't about doing less. It's about clearing space to do your best. When you reduce cognitive friction, you create the conditions for clarity, creativity and sustained high performance.

Prime: Getting mentally ready for high-pressure moments

High performers don't show up and hope during high-pressure moments; instead, they prepare with intention. Whether the moment is leading a big meeting, pitching to stakeholders or delivering a keynote, Cognitive Athletes approach it with clarity, calm and control. Their confidence is built through consistent mental preparation.

In stressful situations, the brain defaults to habit not potential. Adrenaline and cortisol can hijack thinking, tighten muscles and narrow focus. That's why priming matters. By rehearsing a scenario through visualisation, mental walkthroughs or pre-performance routines, you shift from reaction to readiness.

Elite performers use this all the time. Athletes visualise the game. Speakers run through their opening lines. Leaders rehearse tough conversations. They also use physical cues such as breathing, posture or a repeated phrase to anchor their mindset.

This ability to perform under pressure isn't just natural; it's also trained. With practice, anyone can build rituals that reduce nerves, enhance focus and unlock peak performance exactly when it's needed most.

The three components of prioritising are:

1. Rehearse under realistic conditions.

2. Use visualisation to train confidence.

3. Develop a pre-performance ritual.

These components are also shown in the following figure.

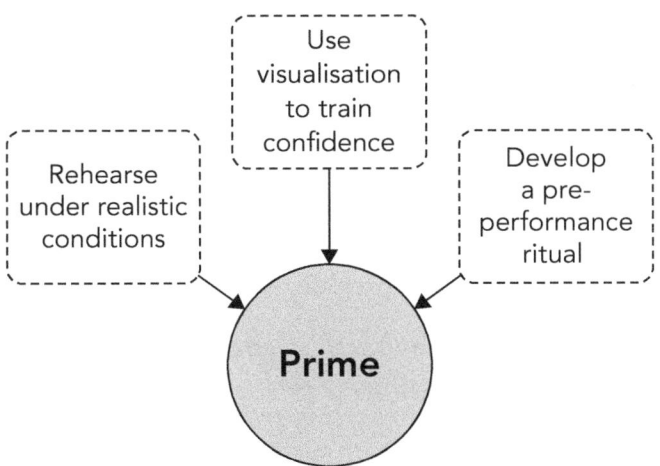

The three components of the prime element

Rehearse under realistic conditions

The brain thrives on familiarity. The more a situation has been experienced before, even in rehearsal, the less intimidating it becomes. When you simulate an event in advance, you build mental blueprints that the brain can follow when the stakes are high. This is why mental and physical rehearsal under realistic conditions dramatically improves performance under pressure. Research by James Driskell and colleagues confirms that simulation-based training (also known as stress training) significantly enhances confidence, competence and composure in high-stakes environments.

High performers don't just run through notes in their head; they practice the way they plan to perform. They rehearse in context. If they're preparing for a speech, they stand up, use their gestures, speak aloud and simulate the room. If it's a presentation, they practise with the actual slide deck, using the real tech setup and timing constraints. The goal isn't perfection but familiarity.

Personally, I go by the 'rule of 7': I rehearse it seven times. This way, by the time you hit delivery number eight — the real thing — it feels so familiar that you can relax into it. You're not guessing or scrambling; you're executing from muscle memory.

When professionals train under pressure, their brains adapt, making the real event feel like just another practice round. Instead of feeling overwhelmed, they step in with calmness, clarity and control.

Use the following strategies to prepare effectively:

- *Practise as if it's real:* Stand up, use gestures and speak out loud, rather than just reviewing material passively.

- *Increase pressure gradually:* Start rehearsing privately, and then add an audience (such as colleagues, mentors) to simulate real-world stakes.

- *Refine with feedback:* Record practice sessions and review them critically or seek external input to identify areas for improvement.

Use visualisation to train confidence

The brain doesn't differentiate that much between real experience and vividly imagined scenarios. In fact, studies show that mental rehearsal activates the same neural pathways as physical performance, making visualisation a powerful tool for improving confidence, execution and composure under pressure. Research by Aymeric Guillot and Christian Collet, for example, confirms that mental imagery can enhance motor and cognitive performance by priming the brain for action before it happens.

Cognitive Athletes use this to their advantage. They don't just imagine the outcome but also mentally rehearse the entire performance. They see themselves entering the room with confidence, speaking with clarity and handling challenges with ease. Instead of simple wishful thinking, this is a mental dry run. The more the brain experiences success in advance, the more comfortable and automatic the real event becomes.

In my own work, I use visualisation before major keynotes and negotiations. I walk through every step: how I'll greet the room, how I'll respond if someone pushes back, and how I'll feel at the end. By the time I step into the actual moment, it feels familiar rather than frightening.

Top athletes, performers and executives swear by this practice. It's been used to win Olympic gold, deliver unforgettable speeches and remain steady in crisis. As Jim Taylor and Gregory Wilson point out in *Applying Sport Psychology: Four Perspectives*, mental imagery isn't just useful; it's a core component of elite preparation.

Here's how to leverage visualisation:

- *Close your eyes and mentally walk through the performance:* See yourself speaking with confidence, responding with clarity and controlling the room.

- *Visualise handling challenges smoothly:* Anticipate potential obstacles and rehearse how you'll navigate them.

- *Repeat before big events:* The more you mentally prime for success, the more natural and automatic it becomes.

Develop a pre-performance ritual

Every elite performer, from Olympic athletes to top CEOs, relies on pre-performance rituals. While these routines vary from person to person, their purpose is the same: to sharpen focus, calm nerves and trigger peak mental readiness. According to sports psychologist Dr Patrick Cohn, these rituals signal to the brain to shift into execution mode, creating a psychological anchor of confidence and control.

Tony Robbins, for example, has a ritual before every seminar. He bounces on a mini trampoline, performs a series of breathing exercises and claps his hands in a specific rhythm. To an outsider, these activities might seem odd. But for Robbins, they are a reliable way to ignite energy and enter a peak state. The specific movement doesn't really matter—training the body and mind to work in sync does.

The power of rituals lies in repetition. When practised consistently, even a short routine becomes a trigger for presence and performance. Whether it is a deep breath, a visualisation exercise, a physical movement or a short phrase repeated silently, these habits help create emotional stability under pressure.

This is not about superstition or performance hacks, but about state management. High-pressure situations often bring unpredictability, but rituals provide a sense of structure. They ground you.

Cognitive Athletes use rituals to steady the nerves, narrow attention and show up ready. Over time, these simple cues tell your brain, 'I've been here before, I'm ready'.

When your pre-performance ritual is locked in, execution becomes smoother, faster and far more consistent.

Try the following to create an effective pre-performance ritual:

- Choose two to three simple actions that centre or energise you.

- Keep the ritual brief—one to three minutes max.

- Repeat it consistently before high-pressure moments.

Reflection and action: Prime yourself for performance mode

Self-check questions:

- Do I go into high-stakes situations with a clear mental and physical preparation routine?
- Have I practised under conditions that mirror the real moment?
- What mental picture am I feeding myself before a big event—success or uncertainty?

Try this:

- Choose an upcoming performance moment (such as a presentation, meeting or decision) and rehearse it out loud, in real time.
- Close your eyes and visualise walking through that moment confident, composed and successful.
- Create a two-minute ritual (for example, breathwork, a cue phrase or a posture reset) and use it before your next high-stakes task.

Performance under pressure is never accidental. It's engineered mentally, emotionally and intentionally.

David's executive use of the Transition Phase

David had recently stepped into the role of chief operating officer at a large RSL club. With decades of experience in hospitality operations and a reputation for getting things done, he came in with a clear view of what needed to change and fast.

But his strength became his stumbling block.

David was action-oriented, direct and hands-on—a classic results-driven leader. He expected results quickly and often led from the front, spending long hours on the floor supervising supervisors who were supervising staff. Despite being second-in-command, he operated more like a frontline manager than a strategic executive.

(continued)

The breaking point

David's passion for improvement quickly turned into overwhelm. He was highly stressed, frustrated by delays and exhausted from trying to do everything himself. From rosters to menus to compliance checks, he had a hand in it all. Nothing moved fast enough. And, worse, he didn't trust the team to meet his standards.

His intensity created ripple effects. Supervisors began stepping back, assuming David would redo their work anyway. Staff disengaged, morale plummeted and turnover rose. His CEO reached out to me with a clear message: We're losing good people. David's work style is the problem, but we don't want to lose him too.

David wasn't failing because he lacked skill; he was failing because he hadn't transitioned into his new role. He was still doing, rather than leading.

So we intervened with a 90-day transition plan. David had solid operational foundations. What he needed now was to shift from high-output manager to high-impact executive. Together, we built a tailored transition plan using the Cognitive Athlete approach for this phase: prioritise, streamline, prime.

Prioritise: From doing to directing

David's to-do list was endless because he believed everything was his responsibility. We reframed his role through the following:

- *Defining executive priorities:* We clarified the top three outcomes David was accountable for: team alignment, strategic delivery and culture. Any task that was outside of those outcomes was delegated or dropped.

- *Implementing the 80/20 reset:* David identified where he added unique value and where he didn't. His obsession with fixing menus and rosters was replaced with strategic coaching of his department heads.

- *Increasing empowerment and reducing control:* Instead of rechecking every document or decision, he learned to set clear expectations and step back. His new mantra: 'If they're 80 per cent there, let it go and coach the rest.'

Streamline: Reducing mental load and increasing leadership bandwidth

David was burning out due to cognitive overload. We rebuilt structure and boundaries with the following:

- *Executive calendar blocks:* Deep-work time for planning and strategic thinking was protected. Team check-ins were shortened and made more purposeful.

- *Decision batching:* Instead of reacting all day, David set two windows for addressing issues and team questions. This cut interruptions and helped him think more clearly.

- *Visibility without micromanagement:* We replaced 'being everywhere' with structured touchpoints. He was still visible, but no longer in the weeds.

Prime: Stepping into the executive role with confidence

David needed to change not only his behaviour but also his identity. He had to see himself as a strategic leader, not a fixer. So we implemented the following:

- *Leadership reflection:* We used weekly coaching sessions to review wins, reset energy and reinforce the transition mindset.

- *Pre-performance rituals:* Before key meetings, David practised being intentional by visualising himself leading with calm authority rather than intensity.

- *Team alignment sessions:* He began each week with a leadership huddle—not to direct every task, but to set vision and empower action.

The result: From reactive manager to strategic COO

Three months later, David was still passionate but no longer frantic. His team was more accountable, his hours were sustainable and the culture had begun to shift. He no longer needed to be 'first in, last out', or involved in every issue. Instead, he led from the centre with clarity, presence and trust. Turnover dropped. Staff engagement improved. And his CEO called the transformation 'a breakthrough'.

(continued)

David had realised he didn't need to be less driven; he needed to direct that drive differently.

His success came when he embraced the Transition Phase—not as a softening of standards, but as a strategic elevation of his role. He learned that high performance at the executive level isn't about doing more but about doing what matters, through others.

CHAPTER 5
Phase 3: Performance

There comes a moment when the preparation is done — the decks built, the goals clear and the vision set. Now it's time to deliver. Welcome to the Performance Phase. This is where your planning gets tested in the real world. Leadership is no longer theoretical but visible, audible and measurable. Pressure isn't the exception; it's the environment. Expectations are high. The margin for error feels razor thin.

Performance doesn't reward effort alone. It rewards execution under pressure. Cognitive Athletes know peak performance is about showing up with composure, clarity and control — and converting potential into real-world impact.

While most leaders instinctively know how to 'push hard' when it's time to perform, far fewer know how to schedule this performance to match their natural energy peaks and troughs, or how to protect their execution capacity with in-the-moment recovery. This is why the Performance Phase blends execution strategies with regeneration tactics. Performance isn't a flat-out sprint from start to finish; it's a series of well-timed sprints, with deliberate resets, to maintain clarity and stamina under pressure.

Many professionals falter here not from lack of skill, but from poor self-management. Energy leaks. Focus scatters. Preparation evaporates. In contrast, the Cognitive Athlete performs with rhythm, flow and recovery. This phase is about staying in the zone longer, bouncing back faster and delivering without burnout.

We're about to step into the arena. But first, let's consider a performance with the highest stakes possible.

Sully's Hudson River landing: The ultimate performance moment

On 15 January 2009, US Airways Flight 1549 departed from LaGuardia Airport, New York. Just three minutes into the flight, the plane struck a flock of geese, causing both engines to fail. With no thrust and 155 lives on board, Captain Chesley 'Sully' Sullenberger had fewer than four minutes to make a life-or-death decision.

The aircraft was gliding at low altitude over one of the most densely populated cities in the world. The stakes were enormous and every second counted. Sully's response would later be studied by aviation experts, psychologists and leadership coaches as a masterclass in decision-making under pressure.

Sully had no precedent for this exact situation. The plane had no power. The standard options presented by air traffic control — returning to LaGuardia or diverting to nearby Teterboro — were rapidly assessed and deemed unviable. Altitude was dropping. Time was running out.

At 3000 feet and falling, Sully made the call: 'We're going to be in the Hudson'.

Rather than attempting a risky airport return, he committed to a controlled emergency water landing in the Hudson River, something rarely attempted in commercial aviation history.

Training over panic

Sully didn't freeze. He didn't improvise wildly. He defaulted to the depth of his training. He had visualised emergency scenarios such as engine failures and gliding techniques throughout his career. This mental rehearsal built the muscle memory required to respond with clarity.

'It wasn't a miracle,' Sully later said. 'It was the result of training, preparation and discipline.'

Here's how these elements came together:

- *Composure as a competitive advantage:* The cockpit recording reveals no trace of panic in Sully's voice. He remained calm and decisive, communicating clearly with his co-pilot and air traffic control while simultaneously calculating glide paths, airspeed and landing angles — all within 240 seconds.

- *Strategic decision-making under constraint:* Faced with limited options and no time for in-depth analysis, Sully assessed the risks and made a clean, committed decision. He didn't chase the perfect answer, but instead picked the best available one and executed flawlessly.

- *Leadership under duress:* As the plane descended, Sully's composure grounded everyone around him, including his first officer, the cabin crew and the passengers. No-one panicked. He not only flew the aircraft but also led it.

Performing under pressure

Sully landed the Airbus A320 in the Hudson River with remarkable precision. All 155 passengers and crew survived. Rescuers arrived within minutes, and Sully ensured every person was off the aircraft before exiting himself.

Post-incident investigations confirmed that Sully's decisions outperformed even computer simulations that had the benefit of hindsight and ideal conditions. His response became known as 'The Miracle on the Hudson', though he rejects the label.

This was not luck. It was performance under pressure, in real time, with everything on the line.

Understanding the Performance Phase

The Performance Phase is when preparation meets reality. It's the high-stakes moment, whether a major presentation, product launch or project deadline, when everything you've trained for is put to the test. The margin for error is narrow, and excellence requires more than effort; it demands focus, adaptability and energy management.

Unlike athletes who train for one event, Cognitive Athletes face performance phases of varying length and intensity — including:

- *Short phases:* Including activities such as a pitch or negotiation, these 'sprints' require sharp bursts of energy and instant focus.

- *Long phases:* These activities are marathons, demanding sustained clarity, resilience and pacing. Examples include a trial or transformation rollout.

The mistake many professionals make is to treat both performance tasks the same — sprinting through long phases, for example, and burning out.

Whether short or long, performance requires strategy. Rather than just grinding harder, you need to show up with structure, awareness and recovery built in, so you can sustain your best work when it matters most.

Seeing pressure as a privilege

Understanding the Performance Phase is one thing; showing up when it counts is another. The difference between those who thrive under pressure and those who unravel comes down to mindset. The story you tell yourself and the lens through which you interpret stress is so important.

Cognitive Athletes reframe pressure. Instead of seeing it as a threat, they see it as a trigger, or a signal that the moment matters. Pressure isn't something to avoid but an invitation to rise. When you've trained well and prepared intentionally, pressure becomes fuel. It sharpens your focus and activates your best thinking.

Central to this is identity. In high-stakes moments, your brain looks for shortcuts, asking, 'Who am I in this situation?' Elite performers answer: 'I'm built for this.'

That mindset creates calm under fire. Rather than wishful thinking, the internal foundation built in the previous phases enables execution under pressure, even in the most demanding environments.

The physiology of threats versus challenges

How you interpret pressure shapes how you perform. You can face the same event, such as a pitch or high-stakes meeting, as someone else but have very different response to them. If your brain sees the event as a *threat*, it triggers stress — which, in turn, triggers tense muscles, scattered thinking and defensive behaviour. But if your brain sees the event as a *challenge*, you get heightened focus, better memory and sharper thinking.

The difference? Control and capability. When you feel prepared, stress becomes fuel not overload. That's why Cognitive Athletes train with the techniques covered in the previous two phases, such as breathwork, visualisation and routines. These habits rewire the nervous system to stay grounded under pressure.

Calm is a skill. It's not luck; it's trained. Elite performers regulate, not react. They anchor themselves with a pre-performance cue, such as a breath, a phrase or a song, that says, 'It's go time'.

These cues create fast access to your best self, helping you shift from preparation to execution with clarity and control.

The athlete's approach to the performance phase

At RAF Lossiemouth in Scotland, I served as a Physical Training Instructor on a fast jet base. One of our most critical duties was delivering parachute landing drills (PLDs) to aircrew, and especially to fast jet pilots who might need to eject from their aircraft and land safely under extreme conditions.

Every two years, pilots attended a 90-minute PLD refresher. We guided them through each step: reaching for the ejection handles, bracing for the blast, checking the canopy, untwisting lines, scanning for safe terrain, trimming into the wind, and landing safely with a roll to absorb impact. We even warned them: 'Leave your keys in your pocket, and you'll regret it.' Many did so, but only once. The bruises were unforgettable.

This training was not only physical but also psychological. Under stress, the prefrontal cortex (your thinking brain) goes offline. You don't think; instead, you execute what's embedded through repetition. This is procedural memory in action.

In critical moments, such as Captain Sully's Hudson River landing, peak performance isn't improvised. It's the result of deliberate practice.

In the PLD training, we weren't focused on perfection. We were focused on precision under pressure. This built the pilot's confidence to act automatically and correctly when everything else around them was chaos. That's what real readiness looks like.

An example of the importance of this precision under pressure comes from Oliver, a fast jet navigator I trained years ago. When he contacted me, he had just completed his PLD refresher before heading overseas.

Mid-flight, disaster struck. 'EJECT. EJECT. EJECT.' The command crackled through his headset. Within seconds, he was launched into open sky, a violent, disorienting and potentially deadly moment. But Oliver was ready.

'As soon as I was out of the aircraft,' he told me, 'Your voice kicked in. I remembered every word. Check canopy...trim into wind...legs together...chin on chest...look under your arm...brace...roll. I followed the process without thinking. It saved me.'

That's the power of procedural memory. His body did what his conscious mind couldn't. It was automatic.

In high-stress moments, the brain's fear response can impair decision-making. But when a sequence is deeply rehearsed, your brain can bypass panic and execute with precision. This is called automaticity and it's the foundation of performance under pressure.

You don't need to eject from a jet to experience this. A tanking pitch, urgent crisis or sudden executive request can feel the same. Rehearse your performances in these moments instead of waiting to improvise. Because when pressure hits, you won't rise — you'll revert to your level of training. Make sure it's ready.

The Cognitive Athlete's approach to the Performance Phase

In the Performance Phase, Cognitive Athletes don't just turn up; they perform. They enter high-stakes environments with clarity, confidence and control, delivering their best when it matters most.

But peak performance requires smart, sustainable strategies that balance effort with recovery. The difference between average professionals and elite performers isn't raw talent; it's how they manage themselves in the moment. It emerges in how they think under pressure, maintain focus and recover without losing momentum.

As covered in the early chapters in this book, many professionals treat performance as a constant sprint, grinding through long hours and pushing their limits. But this approach often leads to burnout, fatigue and inconsistent execution.

Once they hit the Performance Phase, Cognitive Athletes use a three-part framework designed to elevate performance and protect wellbeing:

1. *Execute:* High performers enter deep work with focus and intention. They prioritise what matters, reduce distractions, and access flow states for high-impact results.

2. *Sustain:* This phase is about maintaining stamina over days, weeks or months, rather than grinding through. It's about managing your energy intelligently.

3. *Regenerate:* Top performers build in recovery to bounce back, using breathwork, microbreaks and rituals to reset over the short term and stay sharp.

When these three elements work together, performance becomes repeatable, focused and sustainable, helping you thrive under pressure without running on empty.

The following figure highlights the three elements that make up this phase, along with the three important processes within each element.

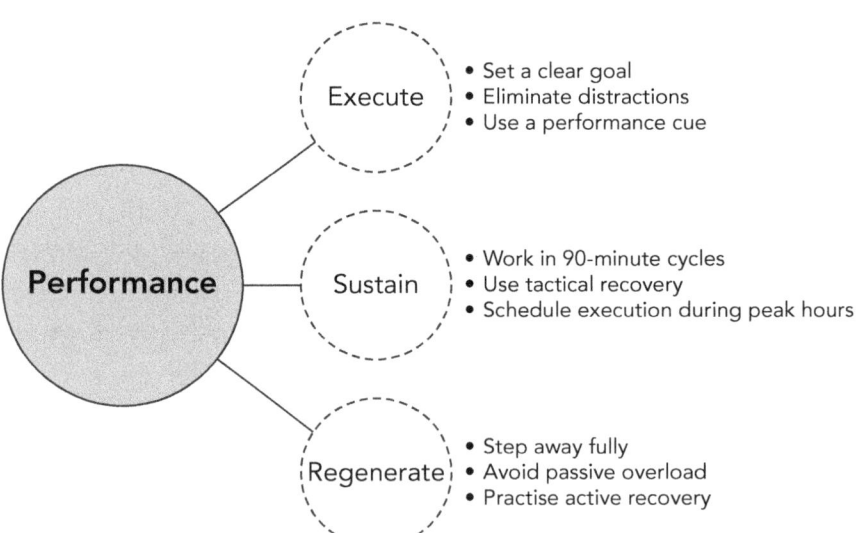

Three elements of the Performance Phase

Execute: Master flow and deep work

When it's time to perform—whether presenting, negotiating or solving complex problems—Cognitive Athletes shift into deliberate execution. This is where focus, clarity and impact converge.

More than simply getting work done, this is about delivering with precision in moments that count.

This peak state, often called *flow*, is when the brain operates at optimal capacity—fully immersed, highly productive and distraction-free. Being in this state is pretty amazing—McKinsey 2013 research, based on a ten-year study, shows professionals in flow can be up to 500 per cent more productive. Cognitive Athletes don't wait for perfect conditions for this peak state. They create the mindset, structure and environment needed to perform at their best, on demand.

As also shown in the following figure, the three core components of the execute element are:

1. Set a clear goal.

2. Eliminate distractions.

3. Use a performance cue.

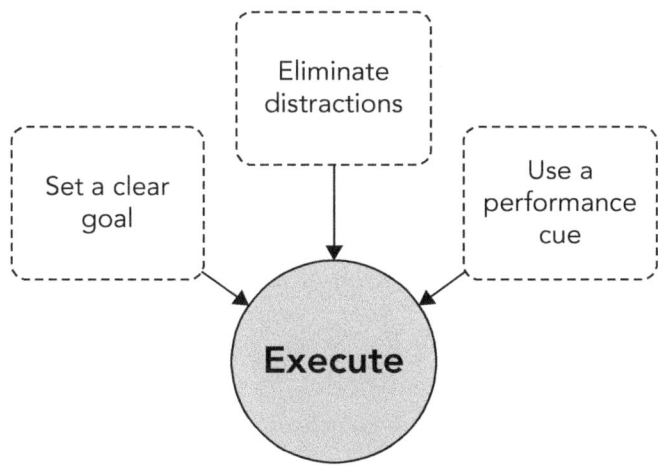

The three components of the execute element

Set a clear goal

One of the biggest barriers to execution isn't distraction but ambiguity. When you're unclear about what needs to be done, your brain drifts. You bounce between tasks, waste time deciding where to start and struggle to build momentum.

Cognitive Athletes avoid this by beginning every focused session with a clear, specific goal. They don't just aim to 'get work done'; they aim to achieve something meaningful.

Clarity gives your brain direction. It reduces friction, boosts motivation and primes you for deep, uninterrupted focus. According to Edwin Locke and Gary Latham's extensive research on goal-setting theory, clear goals enhance performance by sharpening attention and increasing persistence.

In contrast, vague aims such as 'make progress' leave too much room for distraction. High performers define success before they begin.

Think of clarity as a cognitive launch pad. When your brain knows the target, it's easier to stay locked in and resist low-value distractions such as emails, multitasking or mindless scrolling.

Create execution-level clarity with the following:

- *Define the outcome:* Ask yourself: What does success look like at the end of this session? Be specific. Is it sending the proposal, outlining a strategy or finishing a report draft? Write this outcome down.

- *Ask the 'one thing' question:* If you could only accomplish one thing today that would move the needle, what would it be? This question helps cut through noise and identify your highest-impact task.

- *Time box it:* Set a defined window to complete the task. For example, 'In the next 90 minutes, I'll finalise the client report and send it for review.' Urgency and structure reduce procrastination.

- *Break it down:* If the task feels too big, break it into micro-goals. Clarity doesn't always come from knowing how to do everything; it comes from knowing the next right step.

- *Visualise success:* Mentally rehearse completing the task. This primes your brain with a reward and increases follow-through.

Eliminate distractions

Your brain cannot perform at its best when it is constantly switching between tasks. Every time you check an email, glance at a notification or toggle between tabs, you disrupt your focus. A landmark study by Gloria Mark and colleagues found that it takes an average of 23 minutes and 15 seconds to regain full cognitive focus after an interruption. That means even brief distractions can derail your productivity and fragment your attention for much longer than you think.

Cognitive Athletes know that execution depends on more than effort. It requires total presence. Just as elite athletes protect their bodies from injury, high performers protect their attention from digital and environmental overload. They understand that the quality of their output is directly linked to their ability to protect and sustain deep focus.

One of the most overlooked tools in this effort is establishing a *cognitive operating rhythm*—a daily structure aligned with your natural peaks in focus and energy. (This rhythm is covered in more detail later in this chapter.) By mapping your most mentally demanding tasks to your cognitive prime (often mid-morning or early afternoon), and guarding those windows fiercely, you can create the ideal environment for high-value thinking and execution.

Distraction is the enemy of execution. In a world of constant noise, you have to be intentional about building your 'focus fortress', creating an environment and routine that protects your best cognitive hours.

Implement the following strategies to build your focus fortress:

- *Turn off notifications:* Silence non-essential alerts. Use airplane mode or Do Not Disturb on your devices to protect your focus like a high-value asset.

- *Use a focus timer:* Block 90-minute deep-work sessions during your peak focus hours. Or try short sprints (for example, the Pomodoro Technique of focused 25-minute sessions followed by breaks of five minutes) to build rhythm and discipline.

- *Block interruptions:* Close unused tabs, go full-screen, and use noise-cancelling headphones. Visual cues such as a 'Do Not Disturb' sign can help prevent external disruptions.

- *Batch reactive tasks:* Don't mix deep work with admin, emails or messages. Schedule set times for reactive tasks to stay in one performance mode.

- *Work with your rhythm:* Identify your cognitive prime — whether this is early morning, late afternoon or somewhere in between — and align your most demanding tasks accordingly. Consistency is key.

Use a performance cue

Elite athletes never jump straight into competition; instead, they warm up physically and mentally. These pre-game rituals signal to the body that it's 'go time'.

Cognitive Athletes do the same for the brain. They use focus triggers — simple, repeatable routines that shift the mind from distraction to deep engagement. Just like stretching preps the body for performance, a focus trigger prepares the brain for clarity and concentration.

A focus trigger can be physical, sensory or verbal. When repeated consistently, it becomes a neurological short cut, training your brain to enter deep-work mode faster. This process, rooted in classical conditioning, links the ritual to a state of peak focus.

For example, I start each deep-work block by standing tall, inhaling deeply and exhaling slowly while repeating the phrase, 'Clear. Calm. Execute.' This short ritual cues my brain to transition from planning to performance.

The reason this works is because your brain thrives on patterns. A consistent pre-work ritual builds a mental bridge between the behaviour and the focused state you want to access. Performance psychology supports this, and many top athletes, musicians and leaders follow similar routines before high-stakes moments. When used with intention, a pre-work trigger can give you fast, reliable access to your best work.

Here's how to use a focus trigger:

- *Use a sensory cue:* Choose a consistent sensory input, such as a specific song, lighting shift or scent (for example, peppermint or citrus). Over time, your brain will associate this cue with focus and clarity.

- *Practise a pre-work ritual:* Keep it simple and repeatable. Try 60 seconds of box breathing, a light stretch or a mantra such as, 'Calm. Control. Deliver.' The power of the ritual is in the consistency.

- *Move before you work:* Light physical activity, such as a short walk, jumping jacks or mobility exercises, boosts blood flow and dopamine, priming the brain for engagement.

- *Create environmental consistency:* Use the same workspace and time of day for deep work whenever possible. This routine builds predictability and helps your brain shift gears faster.

- *Listen to binaural or isochronic beats:* Both binaural beats (where two different tones are played simultaneously, one in each ear) and isochronic beats (where a single tone is pulsed on and off at regular intervals) can be used to influence brainwave activity. By listening to these beats, your brain waves are made to sync with the frequency that you're listening to. Use tracks designed for focus, such as those set within the alpha wave frequency (8 to 12 Hz), which promotes a calm yet alert mental state. Play them during deep work to help guide your brainwaves into optimal focus mode.

- *Pair it with a clear intention:* Before starting, state your goal aloud or write it down. For example, 'For the next 90 minutes, I'm writing the proposal draft'. This primes the brain to engage with purpose.

Reflection and action: Building your focused execution routine

Self-check questions:

- Do I start each work session with a clear outcome in mind?
- How often do I allow distractions to break my focus?
- Have I created a consistent pre-work ritual that primes me for performance?

Try this:

- Before your next deep-work session, write your single biggest goal for that block.
- Turn off all notifications, silence your phone and clear your space.
- Use a three-step pre-work ritual (for example, stretch, breathe or repeat a mantra).
- After 90 minutes, review. Did you stay focused? What improved?

Over time, these small habits compound into elite performance.

Sustain: Building stamina for ongoing performance

A core principle of this book is that elite execution is not about working harder, but about working sustainably. Most professionals make the mistake of treating their brain like a machine, grinding through the day without pause. But you should now understand that your mind, like your body, performs best in cycles, not in a straight line of constant pressure.

Cognitive Athletes know that energy, not time, is the real currency of performance. I've mentioned already that research shows that after 90 to 120 minutes of deep focus, mental fatigue sets in, decision quality drops and errors increase. This is due to the brain's natural ultradian rhythm, a cycle of peak alertness followed by a dip that requires recovery.

To sustain high performance, Cognitive Athletes structure their work into focused sprints followed by intentional breaks. These breaks do not just prevent burnout but also help refresh working memory, restore attention, and sharpen creative thinking.

The three core components to managing your energy effectively and sustaining performance are:

1. Work in 90-minute cycles.

2. Use tactical recovery.

3. Schedule execution during peak hours.

These components are also shown in the following figure.

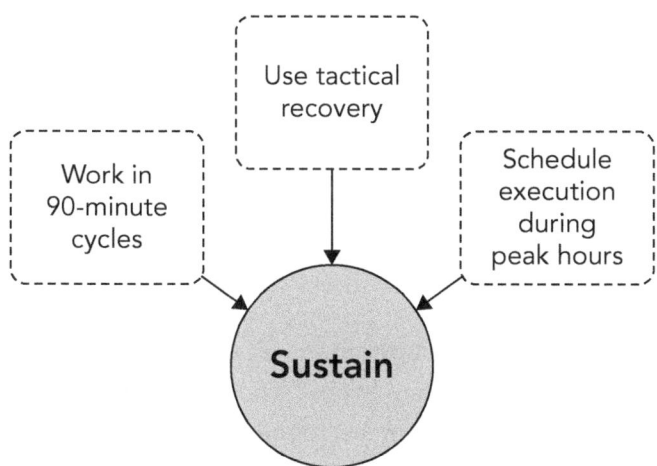

The three components of the sustain element

Work in 90-minute cycles

The human brain is not designed for sustained, uninterrupted concentration. I've mentioned a few times through this book the body's natural energy patterns, known as ultradian rhythms. Now, during the Performance Phase, it's time to dive into the research on this more fully. The following figure, adapted from Ernest Rossi's *The 20-Minute Break*, shows these rhythms in action, and highlights that mental performance peaks in cycles of approximately 90 minutes. After this point, focus begins to decline and cognitive fatigue sets in. This cycle is also referred to as the Basic Rest and Activity Cycle (BRAC), and helps explain why even high performers struggle to maintain sharp attention for extended periods.

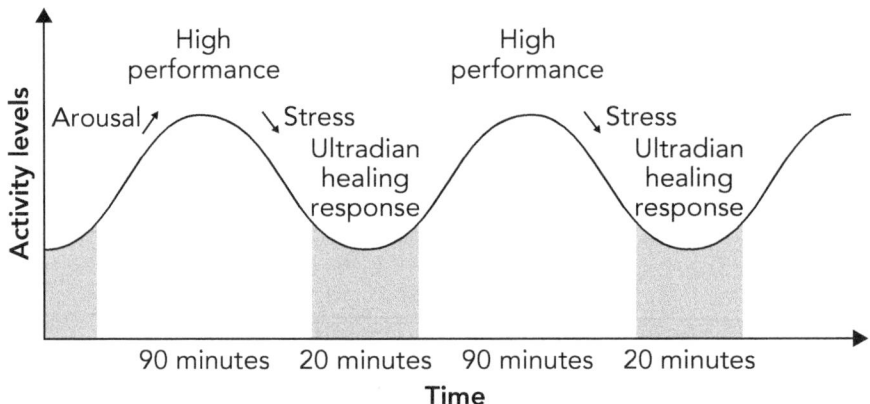

The ultradian performance rhythm

When you ignore these natural rhythms and push through fatigue, the quality of your work suffers. Productivity slows down, decision-making becomes less effective and errors increase. The brain starts working harder to deliver less, leading to mental exhaustion without meaningful progress.

Cognitive Athletes work differently. They align their deep-work sessions with these 90-minute cycles, knowing that respecting their body's natural rhythm results in higher-quality output and fewer mistakes. After each focused session, they take a short recovery break, typically of five to ten minutes, to reset and recharge.

These breaks are not about checking emails or scrolling social media. They are about stepping away from the task completely to allow the brain to rest. A short walk, a breathing exercise, stretching or even quiet reflection can be enough to refresh the mind and prepare for another round of focused effort.

Here's how to work in with your ultradian performance rhythm:

- *Time your sessions:* Use a timer or app to work in 90-minute blocks of focused effort.

- *Schedule short breaks:* After each session, pause for five to ten minutes to allow the brain to recover.

- *Choose mindful recovery:* Avoid screens and stimulation. Move your body, breathe deeply or simply rest.

Working in structured cycles boosts productivity while protecting mental clarity. This approach helps you do your best work, more often.

Use tactical recovery

Building on the preceding component, sustained high performance is not about powering through the day without pause; it is about knowing when to push and when to recover. Just as elite athletes balance intense training sessions with periods of rest and regeneration, Cognitive Athletes achieve more by alternating bursts of focused effort with short, intentional recovery breaks.

This works in Rossi's ultradian rhythms just mentioned, and other science also backs this up. Studies by David Dinges and John Powell, for example, show that even short breaks can restore attention, improve memory and reduce fatigue. These tactical breaks, often just five to ten minutes long, allow the brain to reset, preventing the cognitive drain that comes from prolonged, uninterrupted effort. Without these recovery windows, mental fatigue builds, decision quality declines, and the risk of mistakes increases.

This phenomenon is linked to what researchers call decision fatigue. As mentioned in chapter 4, according to Roy Baumeister and John Tierney, the more decisions you make without a break, the more your self-control, judgement and attention diminish. This is why many professionals start their day strong but struggle to maintain focus and clarity as the hours pass.

Cognitive Athletes avoid this pitfall by embedding short recovery periods into their workflow. These are deliberate resets that promote clarity and emotional regulation. Active recovery methods such as walking, stretching, breathing exercises or even brief moments of silence can help restore cognitive energy and emotional balance.

Take advantage of tactical breaks using the following:

- *Use active recovery:* Avoid passive distractions such as social media. Instead, take a short walk, do some light stretching or practise controlled breathing to refresh the mind.

- *Match breaks to task intensity:* The more mentally taxing the task, the more important the break. For complex or emotionally draining work, take slightly longer or more frequent pauses.

- *Create recovery cues:* Build consistent habits into your day, such as standing up and stretching at the end of each focus session, to signal the start of a recovery period.

Schedule execution during peak hours

Your brain does not operate at a constant level of performance throughout the day. It runs on a predictable biological rhythm known as the *circadian rhythm*, as shown in the following figure (based on research from David Kaiser). Also shown are the typical 90- to 120-minute ultradian rhythm cycles, highlighting the average natural peaks and dips in cognitive alertness. This rhythm is your internal 24-hour clock that regulates alertness, focus and energy levels.

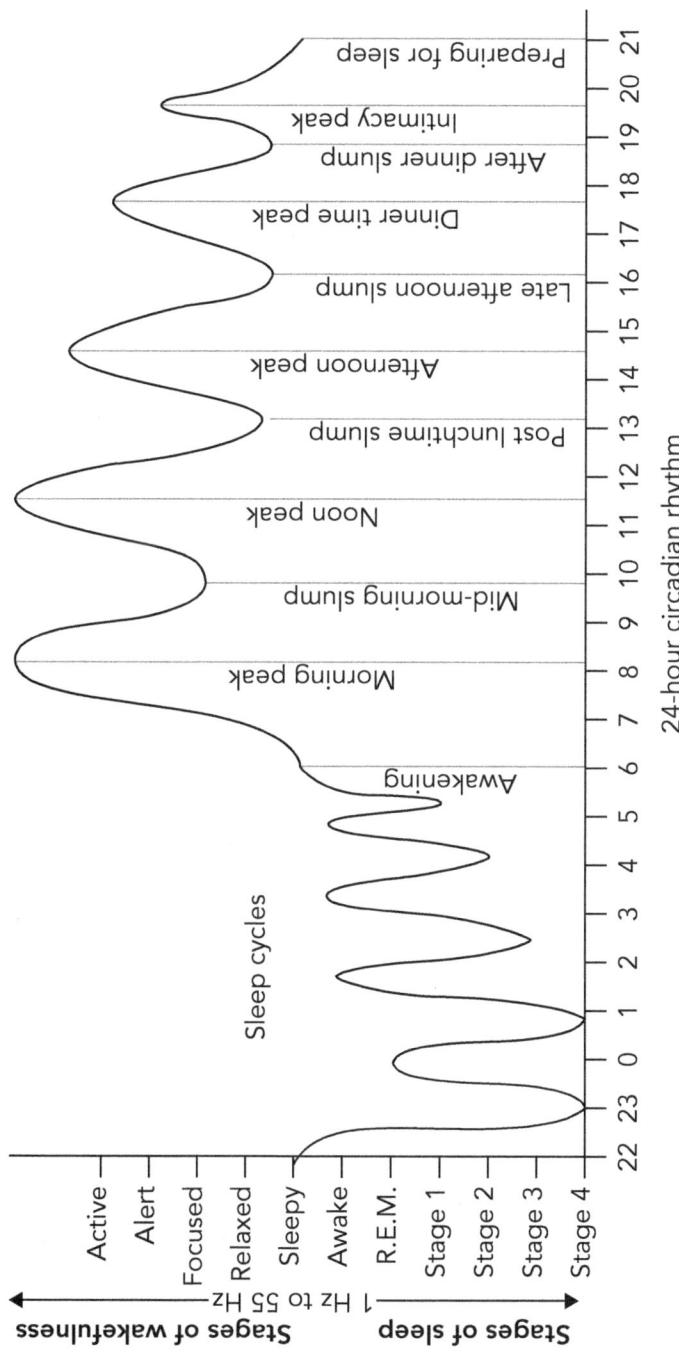

The circadian rhythm, including ultradian rhythms

The cognitive operating rhythm (COR) model builds on this concept by helping individuals align their most critical thinking tasks with natural performance highs and lows, rather than working in a straight-line pattern.

For most people, cognitive energy peaks in the morning, making this time the ideal window for deep, strategic work such as problem-solving, analysis or planning. This is followed by a dip in performance after lunch, and a small rebound in the early evening. If you have ever found it easier to complete routine tasks in the afternoon or struggled to make decisions late in the day, you have experienced this firsthand.

High performers use this rhythm and the COR model to their advantage. Rather than fighting their biology, they structure their workday around these energy cycles, synchronising their deep work, tactical work and collaborative work with energy peaks.

To work in the same way, reserve your peak cognitive window, often 9.00 to 11.30 am, for strategic execution and decision-making.

Follow these tips to apply the COR model:

- *Identify your cognitive prime time:* Track your alertness over a week. Note when you feel mentally sharp and when focus fades.

- *Block deep-work sessions:* Use your peak hours for high-value, demanding tasks that require full attention.

- *Stack routine work later:* Schedule admin, meetings or emails in your low-energy windows and later in the day to preserve prime energy for what matters most.

By aligning execution with your COR and natural circadian and ultradian rhythms, you increase effectiveness without extending your working hours.

Reflection and action: Sustaining your energy through your day

Self-check questions:

- When do I feel at my best during the day?
- What is draining my energy that could be shifted or removed?
- How often am I allowing myself to truly recover between deep-work blocks?
- Am I making my energy work for me—or working against it?

Try this:

- *Track your energy for one week:* Log your alertness in 90-minute blocks from morning to evening. Mark when you feel focused versus foggy.

- *Redesign your workday using the COR model:*

  - Morning: Deep work and strategic decisions.

  - Midday: Admin, meetings and recovery.

  - Afternoon: Collaboration, follow-ups or lighter tasks.

- *Use a timer to honour your ultradian rhythm:* Set a 90-minute focus window. Follow it with a ten-minute active break, such as walking, stretching or breathwork. Do this three times daily for one week.

- *Build one recovery ritual:* Choose one activity to reset between tasks—for example, two minutes of box breathing, one walk around the block or standing to stretch before the next task.

Regenerate: Strategic recovery in the moment

Regeneration is the unsung hero of high performance. While most professionals focus on how hard they work, elite Cognitive Athletes pay just as much attention to how well they recover. In the same way as elite athletes prioritise physical recovery between training sessions, Cognitive Athletes build mental and emotional regeneration into their execution cycle.

As I've stressed throughout this book, without deliberate recovery, cognitive fatigue accumulates. To add to the studies already mentioned that back this up, research by Jim Loehr and Tony Schwartz (authors of *The Power of Full Engagement*) shows that the key to sustainable performance lies not just in exertion but in oscillation—that is, the strategic shifting between high effort and intentional rest.

Cognitive Athletes regenerate between execution blocks to maintain clarity, stamina and composure over long periods. This isn't downtime. It's performance preparation for what's next. Note that this element is similar to the Recovery Phase, covered in the next chapter. However, whereas the Recovery Phase is about longer periods of recovery to recharge and rebuild, this element is more focused on short-term regeneration.

The three components of regeneration are:

1. Step away fully.

2. Avoid passive overload.

3. Practise active recovery.

These components are also shown in the following figure.

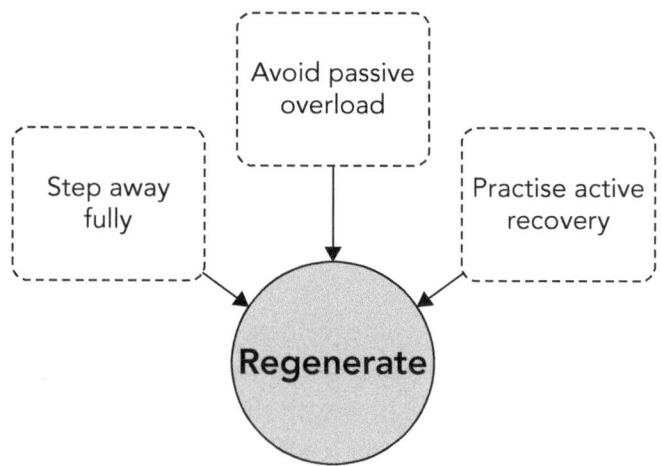

The three components of the regenerate element

These micro-regenerations create the space for your brain to process information, clear decision fatigue and rebuild focus. They are the cognitive equivalent of a cool-down between sets, helping you come back sharper, more composed and ready to execute again at a high level.

In the Cognitive Athlete model, regeneration is a core discipline of sustainable excellence. Without it, your performance becomes a sprint toward exhaustion. With it, you become capable of delivering consistently strong results day after day, cycle after cycle.

Step away fully

One of the biggest myths about breaks is that simply putting your work down for a few minutes is enough. But if you're still sitting at your desk, checking your phone, scrolling social media or scanning emails, your brain stays in processing mode not recovery.

After intense focus, your mental circuits are overloaded. Your brain is like a computer with too many tabs open — still running, but slowing down and in danger of crashing. If you keep pushing through without resetting, you open yourself up to brain fog, irritability and poor decisions.

What your brain really needs is space and stillness. A real mental reset happens when you fully detach, even briefly. That doesn't mean a vacation (though this is helpful during the Recovery Phase), but a few moments of deliberate pause. Step outside. Take a short walk. Change your physical environment. Just ten minutes of intentional recovery can clear mental clutter, lower stress and bring back focus.

Some of history's most brilliant minds knew this. Steve Jobs held walking meetings. Albert Einstein wandered Princeton's streets while solving complex problems. Modern research now confirms what they understood intuitively: movement, natural light and brief detachment restore clarity and creativity.

So if you've ever felt stuck or foggy, know that you're not broken; you're just overdue for a reset. Step away, let your mind breathe and return ready to perform.

Here's how to regenerate with a true reset:

- *Change your environment:* Step away from your workspace. Whether it's a quick walk outside, a lap around the block or simply moving to a different room, the aim is to break the mental loop. Exposure to natural light and fresh air helps reset your mind and boost your mood.

- *Avoid passive stimulation:* Skip the social media scroll, news apps or replying to messages. These activities keep your brain engaged and mentally cluttered. Choose something that clears your head rather than adds more input.

- *Move your body:* Light movement, whether it's a walk, some stretching or a workout, can shift your physical state enough to reboot your cognitive system. Movement helps release tension, improves circulation and prepares you to re-engage with clarity.

Avoid passive overload

One of the biggest traps in modern recovery is the illusion of rest. You may step away from your desk, but instead of truly unplugging, you scroll through your phone, check emails or flick between news sites. It feels like downtime, but your brain doesn't see it that way.

Every time you check a message, skim a headline or half-watch a video, your cognitive system remains partially activated. The mental circuits responsible for focus, attention and problem-solving never get the signal to fully switch off. It's like leaving your car engine running in neutral — it still burns fuel, even though you're not going anywhere.

True regeneration happens when the mind gets a break from input — all input. While you don't need to meditate on a mountain top, you do need to give your brain space. Let the noise settle and give your mind permission to breathe.

Cognitive Athletes treat recovery with intention. They know that reaching for their phone out of habit or boredom won't refresh them. Instead, they choose activities that calm the nervous system and create cognitive space. That might be sitting quietly with a cup of tea, looking out a window or simply closing their eyes for a few minutes. Instead of being time-wasters, these options are performance enhancers.

Here's the key: the less stimulation, the more restoration. It's about shifting from consumption to presence.

Avoid passive overload with the following strategies:

- *Create 'no-input zones':* During recovery breaks, resist the urge to check your phone or open another tab. Let your mind wander or focus on your surroundings.

- *Replace screen time with stillness:* Instead of defaulting to scrolling, sit quietly, stretch or breathe deeply. Even a few minutes of unplugged stillness resets your mental state.

- *Be intentional with your environment:* Choose a space with minimal noise or visual clutter. Even stepping outside or finding a quiet spot away from your desk can make a difference.

Practise active recovery

Recovery isn't about doing nothing; it's about doing the right kind of something. The world's best performers—whether Olympic athletes, elite military units or CEOs—don't just power through until they crash. They intentionally build in moments of active recovery to restore clarity, energy and stamina.

This type of recovery involves light, restorative activities that reset your nervous system without putting you into full shutdown. Try a five-minute full-body movement session to boost circulation, a short meditation to clear mental clutter, or step outside for fresh air and sunlight. You could also listen to your favourite song to quickly change your emotional state, practise a few rounds of deep breathing, or do a quick brain game or puzzle to refresh your focus. Small, intentional resets such as these can have an outsized impact on your energy and performance.

Movement increases blood flow to the brain, which sharpens thinking. Stretching reduces the physical tension that builds up during deep work. Even mild dehydration can mess with focus and memory, so drinking water instead of another coffee can work wonders.

Stanford neuroscientist Robert Sapolsky often talks about the damage of prolonged stress without recovery, and Stephen Porges's work on the nervous system shows how small, calming actions can bring us back to balance. These aren't just nice-to-haves; they're performance tools.

The goal is simple: pause before you're depleted. A few minutes of intentional recovery can help you return to work sharper, calmer and more focused.

Recovery is not a reward but a requirement. It's what allows you to keep showing up at your best, repeatedly. Performance isn't just about effort. It's about energy and knowing how to renew it deliberately.

Here's how to engage in active recovery:

- *Step outside for a reset:* Take a short walk or engage in light exercise to boost circulation, refresh your mind and enhance focus for the next work sprint.

- *Hydrate regularly:* Keep a bottle of water nearby and drink consistently throughout the day, aiming for small, frequent sips rather than large amounts at once.

- *Engage in mindfulness or reflection:* Take one to two minutes to pause, breathe and clear mental clutter before transitioning back into deep work.

Reflection and action: Ensuring you regenerate

Self-check questions:

- Am I truly stepping away between deep-work blocks or just shifting to another task?

- What recovery activity consistently helps me feel mentally reset?

- How often do I reach for passive distractions instead of intentional recovery?

- Is my recovery helping me return sharper or just delaying fatigue?

Try this:

- *Block 10 minutes for recovery:* After your next deep-work session, set a timer and walk away from your workspace. No screens. No scrolling. Just space.

- *Pick one active recovery habit:* Try a five-minute full-body movement session, a short meditation, stepping outside for fresh air, listening to your favourite music or doing a quick brain game. The goal is to create contrast from work, not keep your brain in the same gear.

- *Design a 'no-input zone':* Choose one part of your day to unplug completely. This could be your lunch break, your commute or the first 30 minutes after waking up.

- *Make recovery visible:* Add it to your schedule and treat it like any other performance tool. Protect it like your next meeting depends on it, because it does.

Remember—you don't grow stronger in the grind. You grow stronger in the reset.

Jiang's use of the Performance Phase to overcome avoidance and take control

Jiang stared at his calendar, stomach tight, as he saw the 10 am meeting approach. For months, he had avoided this conversation. One of his team members was underperforming, and while feedback was long overdue, the memory of a previous discussion—tense, defensive and unresolved—still haunted him.

Every time he considered addressing the issue with his team member, his brain flooded with worst-case scenarios: *What if they exploded? What if they quit? What if I fumbled and made it worse?* Paralysed by uncertainty, Jiang buried himself in low-priority work, hoping things would self-correct. They didn't.

The weight of avoidance crept into every corner of his performance. His sleep was disrupted. His focus during deep-work blocks dissolved. He felt drained mentally, emotionally and physically.

That's when we spoke.

'You're approaching this like a chore,' I told him. 'But this is a performance moment. You don't wing performance. You train for it. You prime for it. And then, you execute.'

Jiang was sceptical. 'Train for a conversation?'

'Yes, because if you don't, it will keep controlling you.'

To shift Jiang out of avoidance and into performance mode, we needed a plan. One that didn't just help him get through the conversation, but also helped him own it. Together, we mapped out a structured approach that combined practical preparation with mindset priming.

Here's what that looked like.

Execute: Stepping into the moment with intention

We started by treating the conversation not as a dreaded chore but as a performance event. Together, we created a simple structure to reduce uncertainty and build confidence.

- *Schedule with precision:* We locked in the conversation for 10 am, John's peak cognitive window. No more rescheduling.

- *Use a clear framework:* We used the BIIF model to script his key talking points. The four elements of this model are *behaviour* or observable actions, the *impact* of those actions, the *intention* or underlying purpose, and bringing in *future* considerations and planning.

- *Rehearse to build familiarity:* Jiang ran through the conversation seven times (a concept I outline in chapter 4), first aloud to himself, and then with a peer. Each repetition replaced fear with fluency.

By preparing deliberately, Jiang took control of the narrative before the conversation even began.

Sustain: Managing energy and focus throughout

To stay composed, Jiang needed to manage more than just his words. He also needed to sustain his energy and focus across the entire performance window. He did this through the following:

- *Movement reset:* A ten-minute walk before the meeting helped clear his head.

- *Performance cue:* Jiang used a simple anchor of standing tall, breathing evenly and repeating a short mantra of 'Clear. Calm. Control.' to trigger his focus as he moved into the performance moment.

- *Prime time only:* He protected the 30 minutes leading up to the meeting, avoiding emails and distractions, so he could enter the conversation fresh and focused.

He wasn't trying to 'push through'. He was sustaining his state deliberately.

Regenerate: Closing the loop after the performance

This preparation meant the conversation not only went well but also created progress. The team member engaged constructively, and together they built a development plan. But the real win was Jiang's recovery.

Instead of jumping into back-to-back meetings, or going to the fridge to binge eat, Jiang honoured the moment with the following:

- *Decompression walk:* A short walk outdoors to clear any residual emotion.

- *Casual debrief:* A light chat with me to help reset his mindset.

(*continued*)

- *Mental closure:* He blocked ten minutes to reflect on what went well and what to improve next time.

By closing the performance loop, John protected his focus and energy for the rest of the day.

The takeaway: Difficult conversations are a skill, not a threat

Jiang didn't suddenly become fearless. He became prepared. He learned to treat tough conversations like high-stakes performances. These performances needed to be approached with structure, calm and recovery.

Jiang never avoided another difficult conversation—not because they got easier, but because he got better.

CHAPTER 6
Phase 4: Recovery

Recovery is the final phase in the Cognitive Athlete cycle, and the essential pause after a surge of effort. It's not a quick reset or surface-level break. It's a full-system recalibration—a conscious withdrawal from intensity that allows you to reflect, repair and prepare for what comes next.

In the previous phase, we looked at micro-recovery—those small, strategic resets taken in the middle of performance to keep focus sharp and energy steady. In this phase, the focus shifts to full recovery. These are longer breaks that create complete separation from work, giving your mind and body the space to rest deeply, process experiences and extract lessons before the next cycle begins.

You might have felt the need for recovery before—perhaps in the sudden exhaustion after a big pitch, the blank space after a major event or the slump that follows a hard-earned win. That crash is real, and psychologists call it the *let-down effect*: after prolonged stress, your nervous system drops sharply, leaving you vulnerable to illness, fatigue or emotional lows.

Cognitive Athletes approach this moment differently. They don't see recovery as indulgent; they see it as non-negotiable. Like elite performers, they recover with intention—mentally resetting, emotionally grounding and physically restoring their systems. They understand that performance is sustained by not only effort but also how well you rebuild after the push.

In this chapter, you'll learn how to:

- close out the performance cycle with intention

- build recovery rituals that reset your mind and body

- reflect, recalibrate and restore confidence for what's next.

Before we dive into the science and strategies for recovery, let's start with a story. This example proves recovery isn't about weakness but about staying sharp when the stakes are highest.

The 'NASA nap': The hidden edge of high performance

Imagine this: you're orbiting 400 kilometres above Earth, travelling at over 28 000 kilometres per hour. You're part of a six-person crew tasked with operating critical scientific experiments, responding to mission alerts and ensuring the safety of billions of dollars' worth of equipment, not to mention your own and your crew members' lives. You have no margin for error. Mistakes aren't inconvenient; they're catastrophic.

So, what does NASA build into the schedule of these elite performers to ensure they stay sharp? Naps. That's right. In one of the most cognitively and emotionally demanding environments imaginable, astronauts are not told to 'power through'. They're given permission and instruction to rest. And not just any rest. According to NASA's research at the Ames Research Center, a 26-minute nap can improve performance by 34 per cent and boost alertness by 54 per cent. These results are so compelling that naps have become a formalised part of the astronaut work cycle.

Rather than being considered a luxury, naps are part of strategy. NASA calls this a 'fatigue countermeasure', and it's part of a broader system of managing human energy, recognising that to sustain focus, decision-making and resilience in extreme conditions, you must build in deliberate recovery.

In many ways, astronauts are the original Cognitive Athletes. They aren't just physically fit; they're also trained to manage stress, regulate emotion and maintain mental sharpness under pressure. And structured rest, particularly short, strategic naps, are one of the secret weapons in their toolkit.

Now let's contrast that with corporate life on Earth. How often do you ignore your body's signals? How frequently do you skip breaks, push through the afternoon slump, or pride yourself on back-to-back meetings with no time to breathe? Too many professionals wear exhaustion like a badge of honour, despite overwhelming evidence that chronic fatigue leads to poor decisions, reduced creativity and long-term burnout.

The takeaway is clear: high performers not only push harder but also recover smarter.

NASA's nap culture isn't just a quirky anecdote. It's a wake-up call. If some of the world's most elite professionals operating in life-or-death environments prioritise rest, why wouldn't you? Especially when research continues to show that short breaks, mental pauses and, yes, naps, significantly boost cognitive function, emotional control and focus.

You don't need a spaceship to implement this — just a shift in mindset.

Understanding the Recovery Phase

Recovery is one of the most underestimated and essential parts of the performance cycle. In a culture that glorifies hustle, elite performers know sustained success isn't about pushing harder. It's about knowing when to pause, reset and return stronger.

This is the Recovery Phase, and it's not about switching off but switching gears. Recovery isn't laziness; it's a deliberate, strategic decision to restore clarity, composure and energy after high output. You don't rest to relax. You recover to regenerate.

Elite athletes don't jump into the next session after a big match. They decompress — hydrating, stretching and reflecting, for example — because growth happens in recovery, not just effort. Sports science confirms this: without structured recovery, performance dips and burnout looms. The same applies to cognitive performance.

Leaders and professionals face an invisible load of emotional labour, decision-making and relentless input. Many just keep pushing. However, as stressed through this book, the cost of this is fuzzy thinking, poor judgement and eventual fatigue. Without recovery, stress builds, cognitive flexibility shrinks and burnout risk rises.

Recovery isn't optional. It's a core performance practice.

During this phase, you reset your system, lowering stress hormones, clearing mental clutter and allowing creativity to surface. Research shows the brain makes better connections during downtime than in focused work. You've likely noticed yourself that breakthroughs often come during a walk, in the shower or while doing nothing at all.

Rather than a luxury, recover is what makes consistent, high-quality output possible. When it's skipped, focus erodes, irritability grows and motivation dips — not because you've lost your edge, but because you've failed to recharge it.

Top performers work in bursts and then recover. They understand that output without input leads to burnout, and that success isn't about endurance but about rhythm.

Recovery doesn't require a retreat. It could be a quiet day post-project, a few nights of quality sleep, time outdoors or simply space to recalibrate. The point is to step out of performance mode long enough to reset.

Done well, recovery becomes your competitive advantage. It gives you stamina, clarity and emotional steadiness where others burn out.

In the end, the real question isn't, 'How hard can you push?' but, 'How well can you recover?'

Recovery for athletes and military personnel

For professional athletes, recovery is a critical part of high performance. After intense competition or training, athletes follow structured routines to restore energy, repair the body and protect their ability to perform over time. These practices include:

- *Physical recovery:* Stretching, massage, hydration and deep sleep to reduce inflammation and promote cellular repair.

- *Active recovery:* Low-intensity movement such as swimming, walking or yoga to keep circulation flowing without adding further strain.

- *Mental recovery:* Reflection, mindfulness and debriefing to recalibrate focus and process stress.

The goal of this recovery isn't just to rest but to reset the entire system. Without it, performance declines, injury risk rises and mental sharpness fades. During my time with professional teams, I saw how recovery extended beyond the physical. Team walks, shared meals and playful rituals helped these elite athletes decompress emotionally and rebuild cohesion after high-stakes events.

But the most powerful example I've witnessed came from the military. In 2007, I was based at a forward operating post in Qatar, supporting British troops returning from operations in Iraq and Afghanistan. After six months in high-threat environments, soldiers were physically and emotionally drained. At that time, decompression wasn't standard, and most soldiers just wanted to get home.

But the data from missing this process was alarming. Studies from the United Kingdom's King's Centre for Military Health Research linked direct solider return to higher rates of PTSD, family conflict and poor reintegration.

Together with the battalion commander, we trialled a decompression phase: a three-day buffer that included physical activity, peer support, rest and access to psychological care. Though initially met with resistance, the results were soon clear: soldiers returned home more grounded and better equipped for the emotional shift.

That pilot helped shape what is now formal military practice. Today, decompression is part of the deployment cycle, designed to help the nervous system downregulate after sustained stress.

This experience highlights a universal truth: recovery is not only physical but also mental, emotional and social. Done well, it protects against the invisible injuries that appear long after the pressure subsides.

Whether you're leaving a battlefield or a boardroom, recovery must be intentional—because how you exit one high-performance phase shapes how you enter the next.

The science of recovery

Sustainable performance rests on one truth: the brain and body are biological systems, not machines. They thrive in cycles of effort and renewal. Recovery isn't soft science; it's deeply rooted in neuroscience, physiology and performance psychology. Let's take a quick look at what the research reveals about the benefits of recovery.

Mental restoration: Your brain on recovery

The prefrontal cortex, your brain's centre for decision-making and focus, fatigues under constant demand. EEG and fMRI studies show that even short breaks help restore brainwave stability and executive function, improving attention and insight.

During downtime, the default mode network (DMN) activates, supporting memory consolidation, creativity and emotional regulation.

Without this mental recovery, cognitive flexibility declines, impairing clarity and problem-solving.

Hormonal reset: Cortisol and stress

Cortisol helps in short bursts but becomes harmful when chronically elevated, weakening immunity, clouding thinking and destabilising mood. Recovery tools such as quality sleep, movement and mindfulness help bring cortisol levels back to balance.

Stress is also physical — it can be seen and felt in clenched jaws, tight shoulders and shallow breathing, for example. These symptoms drain energy. Gentle movement, laughter and breathwork help discharge tension, acting as resets for the nervous system.

HRV: Your recovery dashboard

Heart rate variability (HRV), the variation in time between heartbeats, is a top indicator of recovery readiness. High HRV is widely believed to reflect activity from the parasympathetic nervous system — responsible for stimulating the 'rest and digest' activities that occur when the body is at rest and not stressed. In other words, high HRV can mean increased adaptability and balance. Athletes use it to pace performance, and so can Cognitive Athletes.

Immune function and the let-down effect

Feeling sick after a big push? That's the let-down effect. Prolonged stress suppresses your immune system and, when pressure lifts, your defences crash. Structured recovery buffers this rebound and strengthens long-term immunity.

Sleep: The master reset

Sleep is the foundation for all recovery. During deep sleep, your brain clears waste, resets neurotransmitters and processes emotions. Professor Matthew Walker's research, outlined in *Why We Sleep: Unlocking the Power of Sleep and Dreams*, shows that even one hour less sleep can reduce immune function by up to 70 per cent. For high performers, sleep isn't downtime; it's essential upkeep.

Science backs what elite performers know: performance without recovery leads to burnout. Build rhythm into your work. Whether it's a nap, a walk or a solid night's sleep, recovery is how you reset, rebuild and stay ready for what's next.

How Cognitive Athletes recover effectively

Recovery isn't a one-size-fits-all process but a high-performance habit rooted in self-awareness. Whether through solitude, movement, sleep or stillness, effective recovery starts with understanding what truly restores you. The most resilient performers recognise their unique energy patterns and design recovery around them with intention.

Cognitive Athletes push hard and pause strategically. In a culture that equates busyness with success, recovery is often seen as indulgent. But elite performers and science both say otherwise.

You don't burn out from working hard. You burn out from not recovering hard enough. Elite athletes follow structured cycles of exertion and rest not by preference, but by necessity. Cognitive Athletes apply the same principle: consistent high performance requires built-in recovery, not reactive rest.

You too can make recovery work in your world by designing a proactive rhythm that restores energy, builds resilience and sustains your edge.

The Recovery Phase consists of three elements:

1. *Reset:* Step away fully to prevent cognitive overload.

2. *Recharge:* Restore clarity through breathwork, rest and movement.

3. *Rebuild:* Reflect, learn and recover deeply for your next performance cycle.

Recovery isn't a break from performance; it's what makes performance possible. Let's explore how.

The following figure highlights the three elements that make up this phase, along with the three important processes within each element.

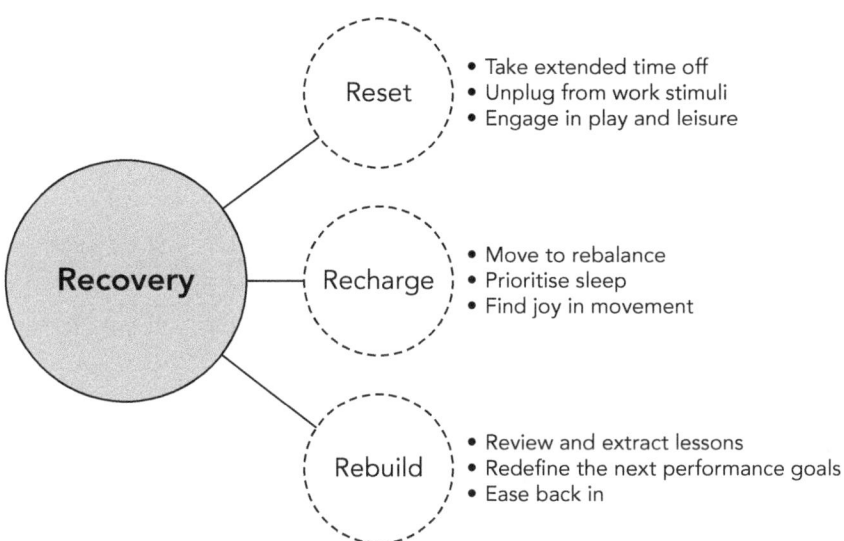

Three elements of the Recovery Phase

Reset: Create space for cognitive clarity

One of the most underrated performance strategies is knowing when to step away. High achievers often push through, but Cognitive Athletes understand that sustained performance requires strategic pauses. Resetting isn't retreating but refuelling.

When you move from one high-demand task to the next without rest, your system stays in overdrive. This wears down focus, heightens stress and weakens immunity. A proper reset involves full mental and emotional detachment so your nervous system can shift out of high alert and begin to restore.

Instead of waiting to burn out, top performers reset regularly. Like a runner pacing between sprints, recovery fuels the next surge.

As also shown in the following figure, the three core components of fully resetting after a period of peak execution are:

1. Take extended time off.

2. Unplug from work stimuli.

3. Engage in play and leisure.

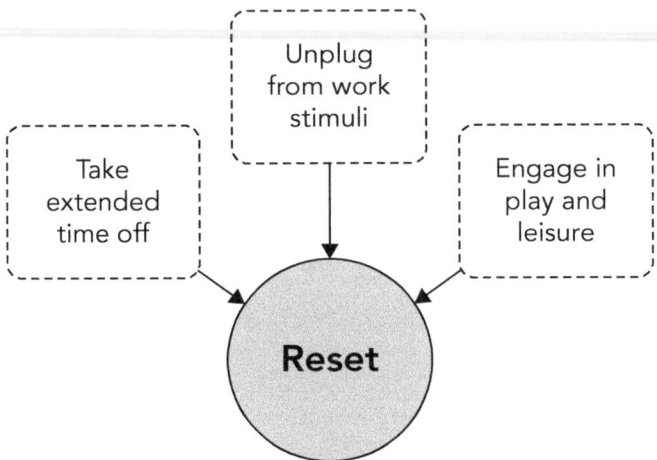

The three components of the reset element

A deliberate reset using these strategies sharpens your edge and supports long-term peak performance.

Take extended time off

High performers often pride themselves on their ability to push through. However, true endurance isn't about constant output; it's about knowing when to pause so you can consistently perform at your best. For Cognitive Athletes, extended time off isn't a luxury but a core part of their performance cycle.

Elite athletes don't train at full capacity year-round. They follow structured cycles — incorporating off-seasons, rest days and tapering — because recovery is how strength is rebuilt. Without downtime, fatigue accumulates silently. Focus fades, creativity dries up and stress builds. You might be present, but your performance suffers.

The same is true in business. Corporate life often operates in sprints: quarterly deadlines, month-end pushes, audits and launches. These cycles demand intensity but if recovery doesn't follow, the cost compounds. Stress becomes chronic, and burnout begins to creep in unnoticed.

Extended time off is the reset your system needs. It helps rebalance your nervous system, restore immune health and shift your mind from task mode to strategic thinking. Whether it's a long weekend post-project, a mid-year break or a recovery day after a major deliverable, planned time off keeps performance sustainable. Without this extended time off, high output becomes inconsistent, and you risk running on fumes. Remember — rest isn't stepping back; it's the step that powers your next leap forward.

Here's how to build extended recovery into your year:

- *Plan off-seasons like an athlete:* Look ahead at your business or team calendar. Schedule recovery time after major projects, deadlines or sales periods. Treat these recovery windows with the same importance as the sprint itself.

- *Use the 48-hour rule:* After a major push — such as quarter-end reports, budget finalisation or a campaign launch — build in at least 48 hours of downtime. Let your system decompress before ramping up again.

- *Create a mini-sabbatical practice:* Once a year, take seven to ten days to fully unplug. During this time, don't look at (or think about) client emails, forecasting spreadsheets or pitches. This is time for you to recharge your strategic thinking and long-term creativity.

Unplug from work stimuli

Modern professionals live in a state of constant connection. Emails, calls, group chats and app notifications blur the lines between work and rest. Even after you leave your desk, your mind may still be tethered to the next meeting, the unresolved conversation or that ever-growing to-do list. This kind of cognitive carryover keeps your nervous system in a low-level state of alert, which prevents full recovery.

Cognitive Athletes know that true detachment is a skill. More than just logging out, unplugging completely is about giving the brain space to power down, so it can recharge for the next challenge. Just as your phone needs to be put on airplane mode to recharge faster, your mind needs periods where it's free from incoming data and demands.

When you continue to check messages or reply to emails 'just quickly', you're reinforcing stress patterns. Even a single glance at your inbox can re-trigger a stress response, releasing cortisol and kicking your brain back into problem-solving mode. That's not rest; it's just remote-working in disguise.

By creating hard edges between work and rest, you allow your brain to stop scanning for threats or tasks. Over time, this leads to lower stress levels, improved sleep quality and better emotional regulation. Your focus sharpens, your energy stabilises and you return to work with more clarity, not more clutter.

Use the following strategies to unplug and let go:

- *Set tech-free hours:* Choose a time each evening, such as after 7 pm when you switch off work notifications. Activate Do Not Disturb mode on your phone and resist the urge to 'just check one more thing'.

- *Communicate boundaries clearly:* Let your team or manager know when you're off-duty. A simple autoresponder or message sets expectations and gives you permission to disconnect fully.

- *Replace with restorative inputs:* Swap screen time for soul time. Read a book, cook a meal, stretch, walk or have a real conversation. The goal isn't to do nothing but to feed your system something different and more nourishing.

Engage in play and leisure

In high-performance cultures, 'play' is often sidelined as indulgent or unproductive. But for Cognitive Athletes, play, leisure and joy aren't optional or distractions, but critical recovery tools. Recovery isn't just about resting. It's about restoring energy, clarity and emotional balance through activities that bring joy and stimulation.

Unlike passive rest, play engages your brain in ways that actively replenish depleted resources. Whether it's a walk in nature, kicking a ball with your kids, gardening or getting lost in a great novel, leisure helps shift your brain from 'task mode' into 'being mode', where creativity and emotional regulation happen naturally.

Neurologically, play lights up areas of the brain linked to novelty, curiosity and reward. It boosts dopamine, reduces cortisol, and improves perspective-taking and problem-solving. That's why breakthrough ideas often come when you're away from the grind, not forcing insight, but allowing space for it to emerge.

I know senior leaders who protect Friday afternoon golf like a business meeting. They understand this time is about more than recreation; it's light movement, social connection and mental space wrapped into one strategic recovery ritual.

Play isn't a break from performance; it's what fuels it. And joy isn't a distraction; it's a high-performance asset.

Reclaim joy as a recovery practice with the following:

- *Schedule joy like a meeting:* Block time for activities that restore you emotionally. Whether it's a Saturday morning walk, a Thursday art class or that Friday game of golf, treat this time like an essential appointment.

- *Reconnect with flow:* Choose activities that allow you to get completely absorbed — where you lose track of time and feel fully present. This might be cooking, mountain biking, building LEGO or journaling. Flow states are powerful reset tools.

- *Ditch the guilt:* Remind yourself that play and leisure are productive in a different way. They increase capacity, not just output. So you are not wasting time but investing in your future resilience.

Reflection and action: Designing your reset ritual

Self-check questions:

- Do I currently schedule regular time off after major projects or deadlines?

- How often do I fully unplug from work during evenings, weekends or leave?

- What leisure activities bring me joy—and how often do I make space for them?

Try this:

- *Block your reset time:* Look ahead in your calendar for periods of peak performance. Schedule a post-project reset day or a mini-sabbatical after your next quarterly sprint.

- *Set a daily unplug time:* Choose one hour each evening where you silence notifications and step away from screens. Use this time for non-work restoration.

- *Plan one joy activity this week:* Book in something fun—perhaps a creative hobby, a round of golf or a bushwalk. This activity is not optional; it's strategic.

These aren't soft habits but elite strategies. If you want to sustain high performance, start treating recovery like part of the job—because it is.

Recharge: Use active recovery to restore energy

Resetting brings you back to neutral. Recharging builds you back up. This is the active phase of recovery, during which you generate energy—mentally, physically and emotionally—so you can re-engage with clarity and drive.

Cognitive Athletes don't wait for motivation to return; they create it through energising rituals. Where the reset element is about slowing down, recharging is about reactivation, restoring alertness, momentum and capacity.

This looks different for everyone. For some, recharging comes through movement — such as a walk, gym session or stretch outside. For others, it comes through music, laughter, quality sleep or time in nature. The key is to choose inputs that genuinely restore you, rather than feeling like another task.

Recharging isn't about pushing through. It's about reconnecting with your energy in a way that feels natural and nourishing. The goal is to feel not only better but also ready.

Recharging effectively after a high-intensity work cycle consists of the following three components:

1. Move to rebalance.

2. Prioritise sleep.

3. Find joy in movement.

These components are also shown in the following figure.

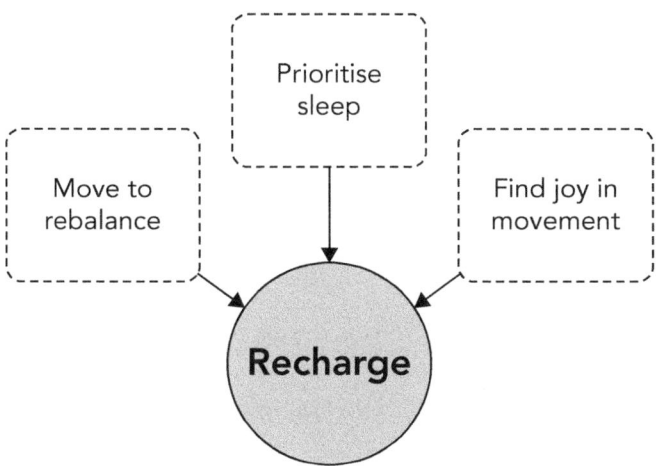

The three components of the recharge element

Move to rebalance

After intense mental or emotional effort, movement is one of the most effective yet underrated recovery tools to help restore energy. But not all movement is helpful in this phase, and high-intensity workouts can add stress when your system is already overloaded. What you often need is restoration rather than more pressure.

Chronic stress doesn't just live in the mind but also settles in the body. Tight shoulders, clenched jaws, shallow breathing and tension headaches are signs your nervous system is stuck in fight-or-flight mode. Gentle movement helps shift you out of that state.

Activities such as walking, stretching, yoga or swimming promote calm without depleting energy. They boost circulation, relax muscles, and release dopamine and serotonin, restoring both clarity and composure.

Movement also clears cognitive clutter. A short walk after a day of deep thinking or back-to-back meetings doesn't just refresh the body but also shifts your mental state, disrupts stress loops and sparks fresh perspective. It's no surprise that thinkers such as Charles Darwin and Ludwig van Beethoven relied on daily walks to process and create.

Early in my career, I made midday movement a habit. While colleagues socialised at lunch — or worked through — I'd run or hit the gym. This wasn't about being antisocial or not being a part of the team; instead, it was how I reset. I returned sharper, calmer and more productive. That rhythm became foundational to how I worked at my best.

You don't need gear or a gym. What matters is intention: move not to perform, but to rebalance. Loosen the system. Boost energy. Return to centre.

Try the following ways to move to rebalance:

- Take a 20-minute walk after mentally heavy work to clear your head and reset your focus.

- Start your morning with five minutes of movement, such as stretching, slow yoga or mobility work, to gently activate your system.

- Break up long sitting periods by standing, walking or doing a few bodyweight movements every 90 minutes.

Prioritise sleep

In the world of high performance, sleep is often viewed as expendable — something to cut back when work ramps up or deadlines loom. But for Cognitive Athletes, sleep is not a luxury. It's a critical driver of resilience, clarity and long-term effectiveness.

Sleep is when your operating system resets. During non-REM sleep, the brain consolidates memories, clears waste through the glymphatic system and repairs neural pathways. REM sleep processes emotion, supports creativity and helps you integrate what you've learned. Skipping either phase impacts emotional regulation, decision-making and mental agility.

Even small amounts of lost sleep can have big consequences. As mentioned earlier in this chapter, research shows that just one hour less per night can reduce immune function by up to 70 per cent — as well as elevating cortisol levels, impairing concentration and slowing reaction time. Unlike physical fatigue, mental exhaustion can't be overridden with willpower. So feeling mentally fatigued or slow doesn't mean you're lazy — you're biologically compromised.

In the military, I witnessed sleep deprivation unravel even the most capable soldiers. After 24 to 48 hours awake, soldiers would hallucinate, forget commands or freeze under pressure. They weren't undisciplined; they were simply human. It was a lesson that stuck with me: you can't out-train sleep debt.

Professionals face a similar trap, trading rest for productivity until chronic fatigue becomes normalised. But poor sleep isn't a badge of honour; it's a performance risk.

Prioritising sleep requires intention rather than perfection. Create a rhythm that respects your recovery and protects your nights — because without sleep, even the strongest performers start to break down.

Prioritise sleep with the following:

- *Set a digital curfew:* Power down all screens at least 60 minutes before bed. Blue light disrupts melatonin production and keeps your brain alert when it should be winding down.

- *Anchor your sleep and wake times:* Going to bed and waking up at the same time, even on weekends, helps regulate your circadian rhythm and improves sleep quality.

- *Create a pre-sleep routine:* Engage in low-stimulus activities before bed, such as light reading, stretching, journaling or a warm shower. This signals to your nervous system that it's safe to power down.

Find joy in movement

Not all movement needs to be structured or goal-driven. Some of the most restorative forms of recharging come from joyful, spontaneous physical activity — the kind that reconnects you to your body without pressure or performance. For Cognitive Athletes, this means reclaiming movement as a source of energy, not obligation.

When under pressure, it's easy to view physical activity through a 'should' mindset — that is, you should go to the gym, should hit 10 000 steps, should burn x calories. This turns movement into another task on an already overloaded to-do list. And when movement feels like work, you're less likely to do it, especially when you're drained.

Joyful movement, on the other hand, restores energy without demanding it. Dancing in the kitchen, walking the dog, hiking a trail or simply moving to music shifts the brain out of 'task mode' and into 'being mode'. As with engaging in play or movement to rebalance (covered earlier in this chapter), these activities release dopamine and oxytocin, neurochemicals that boost mood, increase cognitive flexibility and replenish mental reserves.

One executive I coach salsa dances every Thursday—not for fitness, but because it lights her up. It's her sacred space to let go of pressure and reconnect with rhythm and self. She returns to work more focused, creative and emotionally grounded.

Science backs her findings up—dancing improves neuroplasticity, reduces stress and has even been shown to lower the risk of dementia more than traditional exercise.

You don't need hours to devote to this kind of movement. Small, joyful bursts of movement throughout your week can shift your state, lift your energy and bring vitality back into your performance rhythm.

Find joy in movement through the following:

- *Reconnect with childhood play:* What did you love doing as a kid? Try a light version of this activity, such as bike rides, dancing or even skipping. If it made you smile then, it still might now.

- *Make it social, not solo:* Join a team, walk with a friend or sign up for a dance or martial arts class. Movement becomes easier and more fun with connection.

- *Swap metrics for mood:* Instead of tracking calories or distance, track how you feel. Choose activities that leave you lighter, happier or more grounded.

Reflection and action: Building your recharge ritual

Self-check questions:

- When do I feel most depleted in my week and how do I typically respond?
- Do I have any consistent movement practices that energise me rather than exhaust me?
- Have I created a regular sleep rhythm, or is it reactive and inconsistent?
- When was the last time I moved just for fun?

Try this:

- Take a 10- to 15-minute walk after a mentally heavy meeting and note the difference in energy or clarity.

- Set a consistent digital curfew for three nights this week to improve your sleep quality.

- Choose one movement-based activity this week that brings you joy—not for fitness, but for fun. Do it without tracking it.

- Audit your week: what drains your energy? What gives it back? Block time for the latter.

Rebuild: Prepare for the next cycle

Recovery doesn't stop at rest and recharge; it culminates in the rebuild. This is the moment when energy starts to return; however, before jumping back into action, high performers pause to reflect and realign.

Elite athletes never just move on from competition. They review the game, debrief with coaches and tweak their approach. They do so because real growth happens in the pause, not just the push. The same applies to Cognitive Athletes—reflection is where insight turns into progress.

Skipping this phase can feel efficient, but it often leads to misalignment. You may be moving fast, but without direction. Rebuilding gives you the chance to assess what worked, identify what needs refining and reset with purpose.

This isn't about starting over; it's about starting smarter. It's a shift from 'back to work' to 'back with intention'.

Use the rebuild phase to reset your goals, recommit to your values and step forward with clarity and confidence.

As also shown in the following figure, the three core components of rebuilding for peak performance are:

1. Review and extract lessons.

2. Redefine the next performance goals.

3. Ease back in.

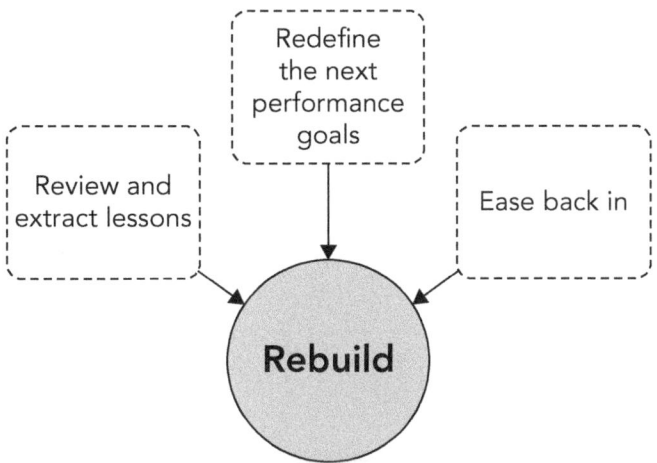

The three components of the rebuild element

Review and extract lessons

One of the most underrated performance strategies is a simple but powerful habit: the debrief. For Cognitive Athletes, pausing to reflect after a high-output period transforms experience into lasting improvement. Without this step, valuable lessons earned through time, energy or stress can go unused.

Elite teams in the military, emergency services and professional sport use debriefs instinctively. In the Royal Air Force, we used after-action reviews (AARs) after every mission, exercise or simulation. We'd ask: What was supposed to happen? What actually happened? What went well? What could we improve next time? These sessions were structured, honest and fast. They weren't about blame but about better performance.

We'd then capture insights in a Post Exercise Report (PXR), a formal record of what we learned. This built rapid adaptation, avoided repeated mistakes and helped us improve across cycles. I rarely see this process completed in the corporate world. Most teams skip it, too eager to move on to the next meeting, project or deadline.

In knowledge work, where results are intangible and effort is mental, reflection is even more critical. Without reviewing your past performance, you risk repeating the same missteps — such as blurred boundaries, poor focus or reactive choices.

A debrief doesn't have to be complex. It can be a ten-minute journal entry, a walking conversation or a short team huddle. What matters is the mindset of seeing reflection as a non-negotiable part of your performance rhythm.

Debriefing closes the loop, embeds the learning and prepares you to show up smarter next time.

Use the following strategies to review and extract lessons:

- Block 15 minutes after a project or performance sprint to jot down three things that worked, three that didn't and one change you'll make.

- Use a shared format with your team (such as an AAR template) to encourage consistent group reflection.

- Make the debrief routine, rather than reactive — schedule reviews after key milestones, even if the outcome was positive.

Redefine the next performance goals

After taking time to reset and recharge, it's easy to slip back into your old rhythm. The world doesn't pause just because you did — emails pile up and calendars fill quickly. But if you return without clarity, you risk falling straight into reactive mode, becoming busy, scattered and misaligned.

Cognitive Athletes take a more intentional path. They treat the transition out of recovery as a strategic opportunity to realign with purpose and return with clarity. Instead of resuming the same patterns, they pause to ask: What does success look like now? What matters most this cycle? Where is my energy best directed?

Recovery often gives rise to fresh insight. Some priorities lose urgency and some tasks don't feel worth the cost. Without pausing to reassess, you risk defaulting to habits that drained you last time.

High performers in sport and business know this well. Just like athletes use the off-season to refine their goals and training strategies, professionals can use this post-recovery window to reset focus, re-establish boundaries and commit to smarter execution.

Redefining your next performance phase doesn't require a major overhaul. Start by identifying one outcome that truly matters. Block time for it. Rebuild your week around it. Choose two or three high-impact behaviours that protect your energy and sharpen your execution.

Rather than coming back with a full plate, your aim is to come back with a clear one—because clarity creates momentum, and aligned effort is what turns recovery into sustained performance.

Here's how to redefine your next goals:

- *Ask yourself what matters most right now:* Identify one to three key outcomes for this next cycle that align with your bigger purpose or team objectives.

- *Align your goals to your current energy:* Don't commit to a high-intensity workload if you're still ramping up. Instead, build gradually.

- *Communicate your focus:* Let your team or manager know your top priorities so they can support, not distract, your performance rhythm.

Ease back in

You've reset and recharged. You're energised, maybe even eager to dive back in. But here's the trap: jumping straight to full speed can undo the gains of recovery. Instead of starting strong, you risk overwhelming your system and slipping back into fatigue.

That's why top performers treat re-entry like a professional pre-season. Elite athletes don't go from off-season straight to match intensity, and neither should you. Cognitive Athletes rebuild and ramp up strategically, gradually easing into focus, decision-making and emotional demand.

This isn't about holding back but about scaling up with intention. Start with lighter tasks, creative planning or short deep-work sessions before tackling high-stakes meetings or complex decisions. Like warming up a performance engine, easing back in means you're preparing for a stronger, smoother run.

Importantly, this phase allows you to spot early warning signs such as energy leaks, fractured focus or reactivity creeping in. When you ramp up slowly, you can course-correct early, and before momentum turns into overload.

Many leaders I coach treat their first day back as a proving ground. The result is inbox chaos, reactive choices and a fast return to old patterns. The smarter ones treat it as a re-entry window, preserving the rhythm they've just rebuilt.

You're not starting over. You're starting from a higher baseline. So ease in and stay sharp.

Use the following techniques to ease back in:

- Start your first day with light planning or reflection, rather than meetings or decision-heavy tasks.

- Block your time in 60- to 90-minute bursts, gradually increasing intensity across the week.

- Use the first few days to assess energy, reconnect with purpose and prioritise — don't just catch up.

Reflection and action: Rebuilding with intent

Self-check questions:

- Did I take time to reflect on the last cycle, or did I jump straight into the next?
- What insights or patterns am I carrying forward and are they serving me?
- Have I defined what success looks like for this next phase?
- Am I easing back in or pushing too hard, too fast?

Try this:

- Schedule a 10-minute personal debrief at the end of your next big project or sprint. Capture what worked, what didn't and one shift you'll make.
- Set a clear theme or goal for your next cycle—one that reflects your current priorities and energy.
- For your first day back after a break, block the first hour for planning or strategy, not meetings or emails. Use it to direct your energy, not diffuse it.

How the Recovery Phase helped Lisa rebuild

Lisa was sharp, driven and full of ideas. The founder of a growing digital marketing agency, she had built her business from a laptop in a café to a 12-person team serving high-profile clients across three time zones. On the surface, she was winning. New projects were rolling in and revenue was up. Her team admired her work ethic. Behind the scenes, however, Lisa was running on fumes.

She did everything—including sales, strategy, operations, client pitches and even admin. Her day started before sunrise and ended long after dinner. Lunch? Usually skipped. Exercise? Non-existent. Sleep? Fragmented. One campaign blurred into the next. There was no rhythm, just relentless motion. And then, it happened.

At the end of a major client launch, Lisa collapsed in her office, feeling dizzy, lightheaded and completely depleted. A medical

(continued)

check-up revealed no heart issues or underlying conditions—just pure physical and mental exhaustion.

That's when I got the call, a referral from a former client who'd seen the same story play out. What followed wasn't a quick fix but a 12-month rebuild.

Reset: Breaking the cycle of constant output

Lisa's first shift was psychological: realising that stepping away didn't mean failure but sustainability. Together, we structured her year into quarterly sprints, each followed by three days off, and a full week away every six months, non-negotiable.

We tackled lifestyle next. With no movement routine, Lisa began the 'Couch to 5K' running program. Even though the aim of this program is to be able to run five kilometres, Lisa's focus wasn't pace or distance; it was rhythm and release. Her aim was to just get out of her head and into her body.

And perhaps most importantly, we returned to what brought joy. For Lisa, it was the kitchen. So she created a monthly ritual of a dinner night with friends, away from screens and strategy decks. This became a vital reset point in her calendar—social, nourishing and deeply human.

Recharge: Restoring energy with intention

With the basics of recovery in place, we focused on intentional energy regeneration. Movement was now part of Lisa's weekly rhythm. She'd jog or walk in the mornings before client calls, and these small actions were delivering big returns.

Next, sleep became a priority. We built a nightly wind-down routine, ditched late-night laptop sessions and set a no-email boundary after 8 pm.

And we didn't just stop at physical restoration. Lisa started noticing how much clearer her thinking became when she stepped away regularly. Her decisions improved, stress dropped and creativity returned.

Rebuild: Coming back smarter, not harder

The final phase was the most transformative: how Lisa re-entered her work after each sprint. Instead of jumping straight back in, we built a habit of conducting a formal after-action review (AAR). What worked this quarter? What didn't? What needs to change?

Few businesses do this. But for Lisa, it became a game-changer. She began setting smarter goals, adjusting her workload, and integrating these priorities into her cognitive operating rhythm (COG—refer to chapter 5).

Most importantly, Lisa eased back in, treating the first week of each quarter like a pre-season. She used this week to focus on strategic planning and low-intensity work. She allowed space to think before moving. She wasn't always perfect, lapses did occur, but the plan was flexible enough to catch and correct them.

One year later: A different kind of success

Today, Lisa still runs her agency, but on her terms. Her team is more empowered and her health is stronger. She still works hard, but now she works with rhythm, clarity and intention.

Lisa's story is a reminder that real performance isn't about running faster. It's about knowing when to pause, how to refuel and how to build systems that support long-term success. Recovery didn't set Lisa back; it set her free.

Part III
Living the Cognitive Athlete way

By now, you've explored the four key phases of performance periodisation for Cognitive Athletes: Conditioning, Transition, Performance and Recovery. You understand that sustainable high performance isn't about pushing harder indefinitely; instead, it's about working with your body's and brain's natural rhythms. You've seen how to manage energy, avoid burnout and build capacity like a professional athlete in a cognitively demanding world.

But let's be honest — understanding the model is the easy part. The real challenge lies in how to live it.

The chapters in this final part are about turning knowledge into results. This is where you can move from theory to action as you apply these ideas in your everyday life — whether you're leading a team, running your own business, managing a high-demand role or simply wanting to feel more in control of your time and energy.

In the following chapters, I outline how to:

- Design your own cognitive operating rhythm, aligned with your energy peaks and priorities.

- Apply periodisation principles to your team or organisation, so you're not just performing but also building high-performing cultures that last.

- Create recovery rituals, strategic pauses and execution habits that allow you to lead with intention rather than urgency.

- Track your progress and refine your approach, just like elite performers do between seasons and events.

Think of this part as your personal playbook for sustained success — practical, flexible and built to evolve with you. A one-size-fits-all approach isn't possible here. What matters is consistency, adaptability and the willingness to step back regularly and ask, 'What do I need now to perform at my best?'

Whether you're doing this for yourself or helping your team thrive, this part of the journey is about embedding periodisation into how you think, plan and act — not just once, but habitually.

By the end of this part, you'll have more than a framework. You'll have a strategy that fits your life — one that allows you to perform with clarity, reset with purpose and lead from a place of energy rather than exhaustion.

Let's get practical and intentional. Let's get started.

CHAPTER 7
Applying periodisation daily, weekly and monthly

Understanding the Cognitive Athlete framework is one thing; living it is another. Sustainable high performance relies on aligning your energy, focus, performance and recovery to avoid burnout and thrive under pressure. But insight only becomes powerful when turned into action and applied in the real world.

Periodisation offers a flexible system to do just that. Whether you lead a team, run a business or work on the frontlines, this approach helps you perform consistently without depleting yourself.

In this chapter, you'll meet Colin, a GM trapped in reactive overdrive, and Dr Elizabeth, a GP managing relentless emotional demands. Colin built structure from chaos. Dr Elizabeth learned to recover between moments. While they worked in very different roles, they were able to achieve the same results: clarity, energy and control. Their stories show sustainable performance is less about perfect conditions and much more about smarter rhythms.

Towards the end of this chapter, I provide tools to build your own performance rhythm. This is where knowledge becomes habit. This is what it means to be a Cognitive Athlete.

Colin's reset: From hustle to high performance

Colin was a general manager at a large, multi-brand car dealership, overseeing five automotive marques across new and used sales, service, parts, fleet, warranty, finance admin, HR and marketing. His office was planted right on the showroom floor — open-plan and high-traffic — and meant he was constantly interrupted. Sales consultants constantly dropped in with questions, updates or escalations. Times that by five brands, and you get the gist.

Realising change was needed

Colin's days began with sales huddles, targets to set and deals to close. Then it was onto service reviews, looking at technician productivity, efficiency targets, bookings backlog and customer complaints. The parts team then needed direction on stock management and supplier issues. Marketing had five different campaigns to coordinate. HR, finance and compliance all demanded attention next. Throw in calls, emails and pressure from the CEO, and Colin was running on adrenaline the whole day.

At home, the pace didn't let up. Evenings meant catching up on reports, prepping for the next day and responding to late-night texts from department heads. Exercise vanished, sleep was patchy and nutrition came in takeaway bags.

Irritability crept in. Small issues felt overwhelming. Meetings blurred. Performance plateaued despite the grind. For the first time, Colin wasn't sure he could keep up.

The turning point came when he stopped doing more and started doing different. He adopted a cognitive operating rhythm (COR; outlined in chapter 5) that worked for him, structuring his day around his energy, focus and recovery. He protected deep work, delegated low-impact tasks and reclaimed time to think.

Colin didn't slow down; instead, he shifted gears. And, in doing so, he found a rhythm that let him lead without running on empty.

Applying periodisation with Colin

For years, Colin believed success meant long hours, constant availability and shouldering every problem. But that mindset led to chronic fatigue, poor focus and reactive leadership.

Using the Cognitive Athlete periodisation framework, we rebuilt his approach. Instead of pushing nonstop, Colin adopted a quarterly rhythm built around the four deliberate phases outlined in this book:

1. *Conditioning*: Colin restored resilience through sleep, exercise and energy habits.

2. *Transition*: He used the COR framework to prioritise, streamline and prep for high-impact moments.

3. *Performance*: He structured his weeks to protect deep work, sustain focus and embed micro-recovery.

4. *Recovery*: Every 10 to 12 weeks, he stepped back to reset, often aligning this time with school holidays.

This shift helped Colin move from burnout to balance. He no longer saw success as working more, but as performing smarter. With structure and rhythm, he led with clarity, energy and long-term consistency. The following sections outline his changes in each of the four phases of cognitive periodisation in more detail.

Conditioning: Building the foundation

Before Colin could step into strategic leadership, we had to condition his mind and body for long-term resilience. He was running on empty, and was reactive, fatigued and mentally drained. Without a strong foundation, any structural improvements would collapse under the weight of exhaustion.

As covered in chapter 3, the Conditioning Phase is about three core elements:

1. Routine

2. Focus

3. Energy

Each of the changes we introduced during this phase aligned to one of these three pillars.

Routine: Creating structure for stability

Colin's life lacked any structured routines outside of his daily work demands. His days blurred into each other, dictated by external pressures rather than deliberate design. This lack of structure kept him in constant firefighting mode.

We focused on building stability through simple, repeatable habits:

- *Morning and evening rituals:* Instead of waking up and diving straight into work, Colin started each morning with hydration, a short walk and a ten-minute planning session. At night, he wound down without screens, ensuring higher-quality sleep.

- *Scheduled recovery breaks:* Instead of powering through exhaustion, we introduced structured pauses every 90 minutes, allowing his mind to reset and sustain focus throughout the day.

- *Consistent exercise routine:* We reintroduced two gym sessions per week, making movement a non-negotiable part of his weekly rhythm.

By creating stability through routine, Colin's mental bandwidth increased, allowing him to step out of reactivity and into intentional leadership.

Focus: Strengthening cognitive endurance

Colin's ability to focus had deteriorated. He was constantly switching between tasks, overwhelmed by emails and losing track of key priorities. His decision-making was compromised, and he often felt like he was 'spinning his wheels'.

To rebuild his cognitive endurance, we introduced three science-backed focus techniques:

- *Box breathing (4-4-4-4 method):* This simple yet powerful breathing technique helped Colin retrain his nervous system to stay calm under pressure. Using this for just a few minutes before meetings or challenging conversations improved his ability to think clearly and make composed decisions. (Refer to chapter 4 for more on box breathing.)

- *Above and below the line thinking:* Colin learned to recognise when his thoughts were reactive (below the line) versus proactive (above the line). Instead of defaulting to frustration, he paused, reframed the situation and shifted into problem-solving mode.

- *Change physical environment for focus:* Colin moved his office upstairs to reduce constant interruptions, allowing uninterrupted deep work while remaining accessible for essential matters.

These changes sharpened Colin's focus. He was now thinking more strategically, engaging more effectively and processing information without feeling overwhelmed.

Energy: Managing mental and physical resources

Colin's energy reserves were depleted. He was relying on caffeine, fast food and sheer willpower to get through the day, but his body and brain were breaking down.

To restore his energy levels, we implemented the following key strategies:

- *Short walks outside:* Instead of defaulting to caffeine, Colin took ten-minute walks outdoors between meetings.

- *Cold showers for cognitive alertness:* At the end of his morning showers, Colin gradually extended cold exposure to two minutes.

- *Strategic nutrition adjustments:* Colin replaced vending machine snacks with whole foods (such as nuts, fruit and protein). A homemade packed lunch ensured sustained energy throughout the day.

By making deliberate choices to fuel his brain and body, Colin reversed his downward spiral. Instead of dragging himself through each day, he felt re-energised, in control and able to engage fully with his team.

By conditioning his routines, focus and energy, Colin laid the groundwork for long-term success. He no longer reacted blindly to stress, because he had systems in place to sustain his performance.

With this strong foundation, he was now ready for the Transition Phase.

Transition: Shifting from preparation to peak performance

Once Colin had regained his energy and cognitive endurance, it was time to restructure his work. His days had been dominated by reactivity—constantly responding to problems, firefighting operational issues and being pulled into every minor decision. Instead of leading strategically, he was trapped in a cycle of urgency, leaving little time for the high-value work that actually moved the business forward.

To break free from this, we again implemented the COR that worked for him. By restructuring his schedule, Colin prioritised critical leadership responsibilities, streamlined his workload and primed himself for high-stakes moments. This shift allowed him to lead proactively rather than being consumed by daily chaos.

As outlined in chapter 4, the Transition Phase is built on three essential pillars:

1. Prioritise

2. Streamline

3. Prime

Every change we introduced was aligned to one of these three areas, laying the foundation for Colin to transition from reactive management to intentional leadership.

Prioritise: Focusing on high-impact work

Colin previously treated all tasks as equal. We worked together to identify the following four leadership priorities that would drive the greatest impact:

- *Customer experience:* Managing escalations and maintaining satisfaction.

- *Problem-solving and execution:* Tackling operational issues while empowering his team.

- *Team development:* Coaching and building a performance culture.

- *Strategic planning:* Focusing on long-term growth and futureproofing.

With these priorities as his filter, Colin began delegating, eliminating or rescheduling lower-impact tasks.

Streamline: Aligning work with energy

As you can see from the following table, we redesigned Colin's week around his natural energy rhythms. Each day had a specific focus, helping him manage effort and recovery more effectively.

Colin's redesigned week, based on his energy rhythms

Day	Primary focus	Energy type
Monday	Tactical problem-solving and execution	Tactical work
Tuesday	Customer focus and relationship building	Collaborative work
Wednesday	Team development and coaching	Collaborative work
Thursday	Strategic planning and business development	Deep work
Friday	Rostered day off (RDO) every fortnight: Recovery and reflection	Recovery
Saturday	Frontline engagement: Selling and leadership presence	Tactical work
Sunday	Full day off: No work	Recovery

This structured week ensured that deep work, leadership engagement and tactical execution were distributed effectively. It also introduced deliberate recovery periods — an element Colin had never prioritised before.

Prime: Preparing for high-stakes leadership moments

Colin used to walk into important meetings unprepared, relying on instinct alone. This approach drained him, so we introduced the following structured priming rituals:

- *Pre-meeting reset:* A ten-minute review to clarify goals and visualise success.

- *Box breathing:* A quick breathing technique before difficult conversations.

- *Debrief and recovery:* Short breaks after high-pressure moments to reset.

These small habits dramatically improved his composure, decision-making and resilience under pressure.

By focusing on what mattered, structuring his work around his energy and preparing deliberately for peak moments, Colin moved from reactive to proactive leadership. With clarity, rhythm and recovery in place, he was ready to perform at his best without burning out.

Performance: Executing with precision

With his personal resilience restored and a clear leadership structure in place, Colin was ready to operate at peak performance — not by working longer hours, but by working with focus, rhythm and intention. Previously, his execution style had been driven by urgency. He thrived on action, but it was unsustainable. Long days filled with back-to-back tasks and constant interruptions left him drained, reactive and unable to focus on the bigger picture.

Now, his daily performance became structured and strategic, guided by his COR and grounded in cognitive periodisation, aligning his work with natural energy cycles and recovery needs.

To bring this to life, we designed a daily schedule around Colin's cognitive and physical rhythms, shown in the following table.

Colin's daily performance framework, based on his cognitive and physical rhythms

Time block	Focus	Energy type
8.30–9.00 am	Site walk and team check-in	Tactical
9.00–11.00 am	Deep work (strategy and planning)	Deep work
11.00 am–12.30 pm	Meetings and coaching	Collaborative
12.30–1.30 pm	Offsite lunch and recovery	Recovery
1.30–3.30 pm	Execution and problem-solving	Tactical
3.30–4.30 pm	Team engagement and walkaround	Collaborative
4.30–5.30 pm	Review and wrap-up	Tactical

This rhythm replaced reactive chaos with structured intent — balancing leadership, decision-making, execution and recovery in a way that was both effective and sustainable.

Colin's daily performance framework also incorporated the three essential pillars of the Performance Phase from chapter 5:

1. Execute

2. Sustain

3. Regenerate

Execute: Structuring for deep focus

Colin's biggest transformation was learning to protect his deep work. Previously, his entire day had been consumed by reactive problem-solving, leaving no time for high-value thinking or strategy.

To achieve flow state, we blocked 90-minute focus sprints for deep work and tactical problem-solving in the morning and afternoon. These sessions were non-negotiable — notifications were off, no interruptions were allowed and his team knew to come prepared with solutions rather than problems.

The results for Colin were sharper decision-making, faster execution and the ability to work on long-term initiatives without distraction.

Sustain: Sustaining energy for peak performance

In the past, Colin had powered through the day on adrenaline, caffeine and habit. Now, he matched tasks to energy levels:

- High-focus tasks such as strategy and problem-solving were done in the morning.

- Meetings and collaborative work were scheduled for late morning and mid-afternoon.

- Offsite lunch breaks gave his brain a break and reset his focus.

- Short breaks every 90 minutes boosted alertness and reduced decision fatigue.

This structure helped him stay sharp all day without hitting the dreaded 3 pm slump.

Regenerate: Preventing performance decline

Colin used to end the day completely spent, carrying work stress into his home life. Now, micro-recovery became part of his daily leadership practice with the following:

- Afternoon walkarounds served as active recovery and relationship building.

- End-of-day reviews helped him mentally close the loop, set priorities for the next day and transition out of work mode.

These habits helped preserve his energy and mindset — not just for the day, but also across the week.

By embedding execution, sustainability and recovery into his performance rhythm, Colin became more productive in less time. He made better decisions, led more effectively and avoided the exhaustion that once defined his leadership.

Now, Colin wasn't just getting through the day; he was owning it.

Recovery: Recharge to sustain performance and avoid burnout

After three months of structured performance, Colin was thriving. His team operated with more independence, his decision-making sharpened and his work–life balance finally returned. He had broken free from the relentless cycle of reactivity and exhaustion. For the first time in years, Colin felt in control — of not just his leadership, but also his energy, time and overall performance.

But true high performance isn't just about sustained output; it's also about long-term resilience. Like elite athletes, Cognitive Athletes must intentionally step back to recover. Without structured recovery, even the most disciplined professionals experience cognitive fatigue, reduced immunity and diminished motivation. To protect Colin from the let-down effect, we introduced a recovery system based on the three key elements of the Recovery Phase from chapter 6:

1. Reset

2. Recharge

3. Rebuild

By embedding recovery into his leadership rhythm, Colin made peak performance sustainable.

Reset: Stepping away to prevent the let-down effect

Previously, Colin never truly switched off. Even on weekends, he checked emails and mentally rehearsed for the week ahead. His nervous system remained in a constant low-grade stress state.

We incorporated the following to help him reset:

- *Rostered days off (RDOs):* Every second Friday was blocked for rest.

- *Digital detox:* No emails or work-related communication on days off.

- *Physical separation:* More time was spent outdoors, enjoying family activities or on short trips to create mental and physical distance from work.

These breaks improved Colin's creativity, boosted immune function, and allowed him to return to work sharper and more focused.

Recharge: Physical and mental restoration

Colin had once assumed rest meant inactivity. But real recovery required intentional, restorative action.

We introduced the following:

- *Low-intensity movement:* Activities such as walking, swimming and yoga helped reset his nervous system without overstimulation.

- *Sleep hygiene:* A consistent bedtime ritual helped him achieve deeper, uninterrupted sleep, boosting memory and executive function.

- *Strategic time off:* Colin aligned holidays with family and school breaks every ten weeks to fully unplug and reconnect.

This shift from passive to active recovery helped him recharge more effectively and maintain leadership stamina.

Rebuild: Extracting lessons and preparing for the next peak

Recovery is also a chance to reflect, reset intentions and evolve. We introduced the following to help Colin rebuild during recovery:

- *Quarterly strategic reflection:* Every 90 days, Colin reviewed:

  - What worked?

  - What didn't?

  - What needs to change for the next cycle?

- *Future-proofing:* He used this time to identify development areas, set stretch goals and refine leadership habits.

- *Easing back with intention:* Instead of diving straight into busywork when he returned from holidays, Colin ramped up slowly to avoid burnout rebound.

These practices made each cycle not just sustainable but better than the last.

Colin no longer saw recovery as a reward; it became part of how he performed. With these elements and strategies built into his rhythm, he led with greater clarity, energy and consistency. He now had a system to prevent burnout and a strategy to stay sharp for the long haul.

Implementing the Cognitive Athlete framework in your practice

Implementing periodisation is about aligning your efforts, energy and time with the natural rhythms of your work, priorities and personal life. It's a structured approach that ensures high performance, balance and sustainability over the long term — and not just for leaders like Colin but for you as well. Whether you're leading a team, running a business or pursuing personal growth, periodisation provides a framework for working smarter, not harder. By structuring your workload into cycles of peak execution and recovery, you can maximise impact while protecting your energy.

Here's how to apply it:

1. *Understand your cycles:* Identify your natural energy and work rhythms.

2. *Define your priorities:* Focus on what drives the greatest results.

3. *Apply the four phases of periodisation:* Use the Conditioning, Transition, Performance and Recovery phases to shape your workflow.

4. *Fine-tune your system for long-term success:* Review, adjust and evolve your rhythm over time.

Start with one change and build momentum. Over time, you'll create a rhythm that supports long-term clarity, energy and impact.

The following sections cover each of these four main steps in more detail, helping you apply periodisation to your work practices.

Understand your cycles

The first step is identifying your natural performance rhythms, both in work demands and energy levels. Reflect on the following:

- *Yearly cycles:* When are your busiest and slowest months? Align high-focus work with peak periods and schedule recovery during natural lulls.

- *Monthly cycles:* How does your workload fluctuate? If appropriate, plan deep work early in the month and shift to execution mode as deadlines approach.

- *Daily energy levels:* Are you sharper in the morning or afternoon? Schedule deep, focused work when your cognitive energy is highest.

Action step: Track your energy levels for a week. Identify when you're most productive, sluggish or distracted. Use this data to redesign your schedule.

Define your priorities

Before you can structure your time effectively, you need clarity on what truly matters so you can set the foundation for your COR. Most professionals don't suffer from a lack of time but from a lack of priority. When everything feels urgent, nothing is.

Your COR is only as strong as the priorities it's built around. These core focus areas become the anchors for how you allocate your time, energy and attention across the week.

Start by reflecting on:

- What are the three to four core priorities that consistently drive your success?

- Which tasks deliver the most significant long-term outcomes?

- Where are you spending time that isn't aligned with meaningful progress or value?

Use these questions as your filters. Once identified, your top priorities should directly inform how you design your week — when you schedule deep work, for example, and what gets eliminated from your calendar.

Action step: Write down your top four priorities. Use them to guide your COR. If a task doesn't align with one of your priorities, consider eliminating it, delegating it or scheduling it during a low-energy window. Clarity here ensures your effort translates into results, not just activity.

Apply the four phases of periodisation

To implement the Cognitive Athlete framework in your own practice, you need to apply the four phases of periodisation in a way that aligns with your professional and personal demands. The following provides some strategies.

Conditioning: Build your foundation

High performance starts with capacity rather than action. The Conditioning Phase is about creating the internal stability you need to thrive under pressure. Before you step into high-output work, you must develop the routines, energy systems and mental focus that make sustained success possible.

Here's how:

- *Clarify your why:* Anchor your performance in purpose. What does success look like for you? Who do you want to be as a leader, contributor or professional? Defining your 'why' provides the motivation and direction to guide your habits and choices.

- *Establish foundational routines:* Build physical and mental resilience through repeatable daily habits. Prioritise quality sleep, consistent movement, nutritious food and stress regulation practices such as breathwork or journaling. These are the pillars that fuel long-term cognitive stamina.

- *Protect and train your focus:* Deep work is a skill and it starts with eliminating distractions. Design your environment for concentration by reducing noise, managing notifications and batching shallow tasks. Train your attention with short, focused blocks and gradually expand your cognitive endurance over time.

By investing in this foundational phase, you prepare for performance and ensure you can sustain it. Like any elite athlete, a Cognitive Athlete builds strength before stepping into the arena.

Transition: Prepare for high-stakes performance

Once your foundation is strong, the next step is to align your time, tasks and energy with your highest-impact activities. The Transition Phase is where you stop reacting and start leading with intention.

At the heart of this phase is your COR, a personalised weekly and daily schedule that maps your key activities to your natural energy cycles. COR provides the structure to consistently show up at your best, while protecting focus and preventing overload.

Here's how to activate your Transition Phase using COR:

- *Prioritise high-value work:* Identify the 20 per cent of tasks that drive 80 per cent of your results. Use your COR to block time for these during your peak cognitive windows, when your energy, focus and decision-making are at their best.

- *Streamline your workload:* Reduce cognitive clutter by scheduling low-value or routine work during low-energy periods. Use delegation, automation and batch-processing to reduce mental switching and free up bandwidth for what matters most.

- *Prime for high-stakes moments:* Integrate pre-performance routines into your COR to prepare for critical meetings, presentations or decisions. Techniques such as visualisation, breathwork and anchoring ensure you enter key moments with clarity and composure.

By anchoring your Transition Phase in your COR, you create a repeatable system that protects your focus, amplifies your strengths and sets you up for consistent peak performance.

Performance: Deliver with precision

This phase is about delivering high performance without depleting yourself. By combining structured execution with energy awareness and strategic micro-recovery, you can consistently show up at your best without hitting the wall.

Make use of the following strategies:

- *Execute with focus and intention:* Use your COR to plan focused work cycles — 90-minute sprints of deep work or high-stakes tasks, followed by short breaks. Protect these blocks from distractions. Treat each like a performance moment: enter prepared, execute sharply and exit cleanly.

- *Sustain momentum across the day:* Monitor your cognitive load in real time. Notice when attention starts slipping or decision fatigue sets in. Schedule routine or admin work for your low-energy windows and avoid pushing through when your mental performance drops. Instead, reset and return with clarity.

- *Regenerate with micro-recovery:* Before and after cognitively or emotionally intense moments, such as a difficult conversation, key meeting or complex problem-solving session, build in a micro-recovery ritual. This could be two minutes of breathwork, a quick walk, stretching or a short visualisation to clear mental residue. These mini resets recharge your cognitive system and preserve your sharpness throughout the day.

By executing deliberately, sustaining momentum with smart pacing and regenerating frequently, you create a performance rhythm that's efficient, focused and burnout resistant. This is how Cognitive Athletes perform at a high level, without running on empty.

Recovery: Recharge and rebuild

Recovery isn't a reward; it's a requirement. High performers not only deliver results but also build in structured downtime to restore energy, prevent burnout and come back stronger. Without recovery, even the most disciplined routines will eventually collapse under the weight of chronic stress and fatigue.

The Recovery Phase is about intentional restoration. It allows your mind to reset, your body to recharge, and your strategy to evolve. Here's how to implement this phase:

- *Reset with full detachment:* Step away regularly and completely, whether through a weekend break, digital detox or scheduled holiday. Remember — this isn't time off for the sake of it. It's a performance tactic that clears mental clutter, restores focus and prevents cognitive fatigue.

- *Recharge through active restoration:* True recovery is not passive. Use movement, nature, breathwork and energising non-work activities to regulate your nervous system and replenish mental clarity. Walks, creative hobbies, movement for the joy and fun of it and low-intensity exercise help restore your focus and emotional bandwidth.

- *Rebuild with strategic reflection:* At the end of each performance cycle, pause to reflect. What worked? What didn't? What needs adjusting for the next round? This structured reflection, whether through journaling or a more formal quarterly review, ensures continuous growth and avoids stagnation.

By embedding recovery into your operating rhythm, you're not stepping back; you're setting up your next peak. This is how Cognitive Athletes create longevity, rather than just results.

Fine-tune your system for long-term success

Building a performance rhythm is only the beginning. Sustaining it requires continuous refinement. Just like an athlete adapts their training based on results, energy and feedback, Cognitive Athletes evolve their approach with intention using the following strategies.

Use tools and metrics

Metrics turn intuition into insight. Tracking helps you spot patterns, optimise your rhythm and make better decisions over time.

Consider the following:

- *Energy and sleep tracking:* Notice trends in rest, fatigue and recovery.

- *Key performance indicators (KPIs):* Align outcomes to your high-impact work.

- *Quarterly reflection journals:* Capture lessons, blind spots and momentum.

Action step: Choose one tracking tool to monitor over the next 30 days.

Stay structured, not rigid

Periodisation gives you structure, but flexibility is part of the design. Life doesn't always follow your plan. That's why adaptability, not perfection, is the real skill.

Action step: Build a 15-minute weekly check-in to review your rhythm, adjust your week as needed and reset your focus.

Delegate to empower, not just offload

If you're in a leadership role, scaling your performance means empowering others. Delegation isn't about doing less; it's about enabling your team to do more.

Action step: Identify one task you can delegate this week. Coach the person on what success looks like and give them room to grow.

Protect your focus from 'chancers'

Unplanned requests can hijack your day and erode your attention. 'Chancers' assume you'll say yes, but every yes to them is a no to your own priorities.

Use this three-step filter:

1. Does this align with my core priorities? If not, say no.

2. Is this mine to do? If not, redirect it to the appropriate owner.

3. Will saying yes disrupt deep work? If so, reschedule it intentionally.

If you're unsure, clarify with your leader to stay aligned. When you must say yes, integrate the task into your COR framework, handle it efficiently, and then return to priority work.

Action step: Track all ad hoc requests for one week. Apply the three-step filter just provided before responding. If the request doesn't serve your system, delegate, delay or delete.

Reflect and recalibrate quarterly

Your rhythm should evolve with your role, workload and capacity. Periodisation is a cycle, not a one-time fix.

Every 10 to 12 weeks, pause and reflect:

- What worked?

- What didn't?

- What will I change or optimise next cycle?

Action step: Schedule a recurring quarterly reflection in your calendar today.

High performance is never accidental; it's designed, refined and sustained. Fine-tuning your system ensures your Cognitive Athlete rhythm keeps working for you as you grow, adapt and push into new levels of performance.

Bringing it all together: Your blueprint for sustainable success

Every profession has its own rhythm, and so your job is to find yours and work with it, not against it. For example:

- Finance and accounting often move in monthly or quarterly cycles.

- Sales teams ride the waves of seasonal peaks and annual targets.

- Entrepreneurs operate in agile, quarterly sprints aligned to strategic goals.

- Performers build their energy and output around show dates and tours.

I cover tailoring cognitive periodisation for different teams in much more detail in the next chapter. For now, remember that, no matter your role, the principle is the same: high performance requires rhythm, structure and recovery.

Start small—one step is all it takes.

If this feels like a lot to take in, that's completely normal. Cognitive periodisation isn't about overhauling your entire life overnight. In fact, trying to do everything at once is the fastest path to burnout—the very thing you're trying to avoid. The key is to start small.

With every client I've coached, whether they're a GM juggling competing priorities or a clinician overwhelmed by back-to-back appointments, we never started with a full system. We started with one change—a single adjustment to a morning routine, for example, or one new recovery practice or 90-minute focus block in their calendar. Then we built from there.

This framework is meant to evolve with you. Begin by picking just one phase—Conditioning, Transition, Performance or Recovery—and implement one habit that aligns with your goals. Once that habit becomes part of your rhythm, layer in another. Over time, these micro-adjustments stack up into a powerful, personalised system that supports your energy, focus and results.

Remember—peak performance isn't about perfection. It's about progress that's strategic, deliberate and sustainable.

You don't need to master every phase overnight. You just need to start—intentionally, consistently and with a rhythm that works for you. That's how Cognitive Athletes train. That's how sustainable success is built.

Dr Elizabeth's evolution from fatigued to focused

Dr Elizabeth, a respected GP in a busy medical clinic, knew all the science behind performance and recovery. She taught strategies such as breathwork, nervous system regulation, hydration and sleep hygiene to her patients. Yet, despite this knowledge, Dr Elizabeth found herself emotionally depleted, mentally scattered and physically exhausted. Like many professionals in high-pressure environments, she didn't have a knowledge gap—but she did have an implementation gap.

Her days were back-to-back with emotionally intense consults, urgent decision-making and endless admin. She had no space to reset and no margin in which to breathe. She was functioning on autopilot, surviving on willpower and running on empty. Our work together began not by introducing new ideas but by helping her operationalise what she already knew through the lens of cognitive periodisation.

We applied the same four-phase framework I use with leaders and athletes—Conditioning, Transition, Performance and Recovery—but adapted it to the realities of clinical life.

Conditioning: Building internal capacity

We started by restoring the foundation through routine, focus and energy. Dr Elizabeth couldn't change her schedule, but she could control how she entered and exited her day. We anchored

(continued)

---

her mornings with a short movement and breath routine, inserted a five-minute micro-break after her most emotionally taxing mid-morning consult, and created a wind-down ritual at night. These small routines gave structure to the chaos and helped her move through the day with more control.

She also introduced 'mental reset' moments between patients, such as 90 seconds of breathwork, stepping outside or anchoring to a calming visual cue. These helped her transition mentally between consults, reducing emotional carryover and cognitive fatigue.

Transition: Moving from survival to intentional flow

Dr Elizabeth's day was driven by fixed appointments, so we worked on how she moved through her day rather than trying to redesign it. We grouped consult types more deliberately, alternating emotionally intense sessions with lighter reviews whenever possible. We also reduced multitasking: admin was batched into protected windows and pre-written templates improved efficiency without sacrificing care.

We introduced pre-consult 'priming' rituals, including box breathing, reviewing key notes and setting an intention for how she wanted the patient to feel. This helped her show up with presence, clarity and emotional steadiness.

Performance: Sustaining clarity under pressure

Execution for Dr Elizabeth wasn't about doing more; it was about being consistently present and composed across a long, demanding day. We built in two additional 90-second micro-resets and added short buffer blocks to prevent back-to-back emotional overload. She also kept a family picture and a smooth river stone in the consult room as visual anchors, and used subtle psychological cues, such as tapping her thumb and forefinger while slowly exhaling, to signal a mental reset. These strategies kept her focus sharp and energy steady under pressure.

Instead of powering through, Dr Elizabeth now moved through her day with rhythm, intentionally resetting, listening deeply and conserving emotional bandwidth.

Recovery: Building a long-term resilience strategy

The final breakthrough came when Dr Elizabeth reframed recovery as a non-negotiable, rather than a luxury. Every ten weeks, she scheduled a full week off, aligned with her natural work cycles and protected from work creep. During these weeks, she disconnected completely, walked along the coast and painted—activities that recharged her emotionally and cognitively.

After each cycle, she completed a short after-action review by asking: What worked? What didn't? What would she adjust next time? Recovery became a performance tool and not an afterthought.

The result

Dr Elizabeth didn't reduce her workload or change careers. Instead, she shifted from reactive survival to intentional performance. She regained control of her energy, sharpened her focus and reconnected with her purpose. Through cognitive periodisation, she now leads like a Cognitive Athlete, prepared, present and sustainably high performing.

CHAPTER 8

Leading teams and organisations with a periodised approach

In sport and the military, teams are trained to operate in cycles, with periods of intense performance followed by deliberate recovery and preparation. But in most organisations, no such rhythm exists. Every week is a sprint. Every month is urgent. And, over time, the cost of this is high: exhausted leaders, disengaged teams and stalled growth. If individuals can benefit from cognitive periodisation, the impact is magnified when this framework is applied to teams and businesses as a whole.

This chapter explores what it means to lead with rhythm, outlining how teams can sustain performance without burnout and how leaders can scale their impact by getting intentional about energy, cycles and collective flow.

Let's begin with the story of Mark, a business owner whose relentless drive almost cost him everything he was working to build.

Mark's wake-up call: From firefighting to forward-focused leadership

Mark was a business owner who never stopped. He ran a growing project management firm in construction and, from the outside, it looked successful. But behind the scenes, he was burning out and taking his team with him. He was the first to arrive, the last to leave, and the one replying to emails at midnight. When something went wrong, Mark was there to fix it himself.

But his relentlessness had a cost.

His leadership team, once high performing, began quietly leaving. Some cited family, others 'new opportunities', but the unspoken truth was that Mark's always-on culture was draining them. Emails flew at all hours. Expectations were sky-high but rarely articulated. No-one felt safe saying they were struggling.

When I first met Mark, we ran a psychological safety survey with his team, measuring how safe and comfortable individuals felt within the workplace. The scores looked fine, but the comments told another story—people felt overwhelmed, afraid to fail and stuck in survival mode.

Mark was no different. He wanted to grow the business nationally but couldn't figure out why nothing was sticking, why great people were leaving and why, despite all his effort, he felt stalled.

I asked him one question: 'If you want to grow, what's your plan for stepping out of the day-to-day?' He didn't have one. So we started there.

We mapped his business rhythm—tracking his busy seasons, quieter lulls and natural pressure points—and identified moments when he could step back and reflect. I challenged him to take time off each quarter. At first, he resisted. But, over time, he began to see the value.

I also encouraged him to pick up a hobby. He chose padel, a racquet sport that's like a mix of tennis and squash. This became his outlet—a way to move, disconnect and reset.

Once Mark's own rhythm improved, we worked with his team's rhythms. Each leader mapped their energy cycles, burnout signs and preferred ways of working. We aligned projects accordingly, protected recovery windows and set boundaries around communication.

Gradually, the culture began to shift. People felt safer, energy stabilised and performance improved — not because anyone worked harder, but because they worked smarter.

Today, Mark's company is national, with over 300 employees. But, more importantly, he leads with intention. He's no longer trapped in the daily grind, and is instead focused on strategy, vision and culture — the work of a true leader.

The company isn't perfect. Pressure still shows up. But now Mark recognises the signs early and resets before things unravel. Most importantly, he now understands real leadership is about knowing when to push, when to pause and how to lead with purpose.

Understanding how periodisation can work in teams

Corporate teams experience natural ebbs and flows in workload just like elite sports or military teams. Sales teams sprint to hit end-of-month targets. Finance teams surge during month-end close and year-end reporting. Product teams push hard toward launch, and then enter slower cycles of iteration and planning.

But here's the difference: in sport and defence, these cycles are intentionally planned. In most organisations, they're not. Before jumping into how cognitive periodisation could work in your organisation, let's take a closer look at some of the lessons gained from the military and elite athletes.

Lessons from the military

The military, like professional sport, has long understood that sustainable performance demands more than effort; it also requires the right rhythm. Strategic planning, structured execution and deliberate recovery are essential not only for success but also for survival under pressure.

In 2003, I had the privilege of supporting Royal Air Force (RAF) squadrons during Operation TELIC, a high-stakes deployment to Iraq. One squadron in particular stood out. Operating Tornado GR4 aircraft for reconnaissance and air support, their mission placed them in extreme conditions with little room for error. The challenge was physical, mental and organisational.

To prepare, we applied a structured periodisation model that mirrored elite athletic performance cycles. The approach consisted of the four deliberate phases outlined in this book: Conditioning, Transition, Performance and Recovery. Each phase played a critical role in ensuring the team could perform at peak levels over an extended deployment without burning out.

In the Conditioning Phase, we built a strong foundation physically and mentally. The focus was on readiness — increasing fitness, boosting resilience and fostering trust through shared challenges. Even the cold, harsh training environment in Scotland toughened the squadron for the extreme heat of the Middle East and built cohesion under pressure.

The Transition Phase refined their mission-critical skills. Through simulations and tactical rehearsals, the team practised operating under stress, replicating real deployment scenarios. This phase helped sharpen focus, improve adaptability and ensure the squadron entered the operational theatre aligned and confident.

Once deployed to the Gulf, the squadron entered their Performance Phase: four months of high-pressure operations in 50°C heat, executing missions that required precision and clarity in the face of fatigue and uncertainty. Thanks to their preparation, they performed exceptionally. No heat-related incidents or stress-related absences were recorded, and operational effectiveness was sustained throughout.

Just as critical was what happened after in the structured Recovery Phase. On return to the United Kingdom, the team then spent a week in Cyprus for decompression, engaging in adventure training, physical activity and psychological reset. (This strategy was specific to this squadron, and was before a formal decompression strategy was trailed by the RAF in 2007, as described in chapter 6.) This wasn't downtime; it was performance insurance. It gave personnel time to process the experience, reconnect with peers, and return home grounded rather than drained.

What made this periodisation approach so effective wasn't just the preparation but also the rhythm. Each phase had a purpose. Conditioning created resilience. Transition built confidence. Performance was focused and sustainable. Recovery ensured learning and longevity.

And while the stakes in military operations are unique, the principles are universal.

In today's corporate world, leaders often push for constant performance without the pauses that enable it. But the military shows us what's possible when rhythm is intentional. When teams are trained to prepare, deliver and recover in cycles, they not only survive high-pressure environments but also excel in them.

Lessons from sport: How elite teams sustain performance

Professional sports teams also achieve greatness through rhythm. Behind every championship season is the same structured cycle of Conditioning, Transition, Performance and Recovery, designed to maintain peak performance over time.

Whether it's a football team preparing for the Champions League or an Olympic athlete training for a four-year goal, periodisation ensures that intensity is applied at the right time, and recovery is an integral part of the performance strategy.

Take European football. The English Premier League, known for its high tempo and physical demands, introduced a mid-season winter break in 2020 to help reduce injuries and improve long-term performance. By 2024, the break had expanded to two full weeks, with the season starting earlier and FA Cup replays removed. This wasn't just about rest. It was about strategic reset, with coaches using the time for light training, tactical realignment and mental refresh.

The result? Teams came back sharper, more consistent and less injury-prone. A 2004 study published in the *British Journal of Sports Medicine* confirmed that structured periodisation reduces injury rates by over 25 per cent, while improving psychological readiness and decision-making under pressure.

What makes this approach work is not only the break but also the planning around the break. Coaches analyse the season schedule in advance, taper training loads before high-intensity periods, rotate players and personalise recovery. They don't wait until burnout hits. They anticipate it and adjust before it becomes a problem.

Now consider the corporate world. Most teams are stuck in constant delivery mode. Every week feels like match day. Meetings, deadlines and projects stack endlessly. With no tapering and no planned recovery, work is just a constant push.

This ultimately results in burnout, disengagement and a drop in quality — not because people aren't capable, but because they're running on empty.

What if corporate teams adopted the same rhythm as the military and elite athletes? Consider the following:

- Conditioning could mean onboarding, alignment and strategic planning.

- Transition might involve simplifying tasks and preparing for big launches.

- Performance could become focused sprints with minimal distractions.

- Recovery might include reflection, lighter workloads and energy resets.

Elite teams also personalise their approach. A player returning from injury doesn't follow the same plan as a match-fit striker. Likewise, in business, team members have different cognitive loads, energy cycles and responsibilities. Tailoring work around these team and individual rhythms isn't indulgent but smart leadership.

To begin, build a 'season view' of your team's workload. Identify high-stakes periods, plan recovery time and communicate expectations in advance.

Because in sport and in business, it's not relentlessness that wins championships — it's rhythm.

Corporate teams: Parallels and gaps

In many companies, the year begins in full sprint and never lets up. People run at maximum capacity until forced to stop, usually at Christmas. I call this 'limping over the finish line', where the holiday break feels less like celebration and more like collapse.

What follows is the let-down effect. After months of cortisol-fuelled pressure, immune systems crash and people fall ill. They make resolutions to slow down next year. But by February, the cycle resumes. And that's why sustainable performance can't rely on individual willpower alone. It needs to be embedded in team routines, leadership rhythms and cultural norms.

This is where cognitive periodisation becomes an essential smarter operating model for high-performing organisations.

Tailoring periodisation for organisations

To embed this model, organisations must recognise the unique rhythms of their teams and functions. The following sections outline how periodisation might look across typical business units.

Sales teams: From constant push to strategic rhythm

Sales teams often operate in relentless monthly or quarterly cycles, with crushing pressure in the final days to close deals. Nowhere is this more intense than in the automotive industry, where urgency overrides strategy and burnout is routine.

In many dealerships I've worked with, the target is fixed: sell 70 new cars every month, for example, regardless of market shifts, team energy or season. Every month is a race. Every day is numbers-driven. Little space is left for reflection, planning or recovery.

As month-end approaches, chaos kicks in. Managers push last-minute deals, discounts fly and customers are pressured with 'today only' offers. Salespeople scramble from lead to lead, with no time to build rapport or truly understand customer needs.

This is the legacy sales model of speed over sustainability. It leaves little room for consultative selling, which builds trust and long-term value. What suffers isn't just sales quality, but also team pride and wellbeing.

The consequences are predictable:

- Burnout and high turnover become the norm.

- Customers feel like targets rather than people, damaging long-term relationships and referral potential.

- Sales professionals lose confidence, resorting to discounting over value, and closing over connection.

But it doesn't have to be this way—a smarter rhythm is possible. Cognitive periodisation can be applied not just to days or weeks but also across the business year. Especially in sales, aligning team energy with market flow can prevent burnout and improve performance.

In Australia, automotive sales follow a predictable rhythm:

- Peaks in November to February (summer sales) and June (end of financial year, or EOFY, rush), driven by psychology, promotions and tax incentives.

- Dips in July to September, and sometimes early spring, when market interest cools.

Yet many dealerships push as if every month is December. As a result, teams burn out mid-winter or collapse just before Christmas.

Here's a better approach:

- *January to February — Performance Phase:* High output, riding the wave of summer momentum and promotions.

- *March — Recovery Phase:* Shorter hours, team reflection and capability-building after the summer rush.

- *April — Conditioning Phase:* Prepping for EOFY. Staff train on finance, fleet and tax-related sales.

- *May — Transition Phase:* Lead generation ramps up as staff training continues.

- *June — Performance Phase:* Full execution mode. High urgency and high risk of burnout requires strategic energy management.

- *July — Recovery Phase:* Post-EOFY pause. Light meetings, flexible hours, team gratitude.

- *August to September — Conditioning Phase:* Use the softer period for managing customer relationships, prospecting and skill development.

- *October — Transition Phase:* Gearing up for year-end, stock prep, campaign planning and lead re-engagement.

- *November to December — Performance Phase:* Final sales push. With the right rhythm, it's sustainable.

This model respects both the market and the people. Rather than being about slowing down, it's about being strategic. As should be clear by now, real performance isn't about being 'on' all the time. It's about knowing when to be on and having the energy and focus to deliver when it matters most.

Finance teams: From constant deadline mode to sustainable precision

Finance teams are the backbone of organisational performance. They not only manage money but also ensure operational stability, informed decision-making and strategic planning. But unlike other business units, which have clear cycles, finance must juggle multiple, overlapping demands — including payroll, reporting, forecasting, audit prep, compliance, budgeting, and accounts payable and receivable.

Each function has its own rhythm, yet they all compete for the same limited resources: time, energy and attention.

In my experience working with finance teams, they start with the best intentions, creating a clearly mapped year, with key dates, deliverables and planning windows. But that clarity often evaporates. Curveballs arrive in the form of system upgrades, last-minute projects, extra reporting requests, steering committees and transformation initiatives. A well-structured plan quickly becomes a chaotic sprint.

Finance professionals rarely push back due to a deep sense of responsibility. They know what's at stake. If they don't deliver, payments are delayed, reports are late or compliance risks emerge. So, they absorb the pressure and deliver under strain. But, over time, the cost adds up.

The impact is significant:

- Strategic finance work such as scenario planning, process improvement and business partnering gets sacrificed for urgent tasks.

- Team wellbeing declines. Stress and long hours become the norm, especially around quarter-end and EOFY deadlines.

- Burnout creeps in silently, disguised as diligence.

And because these cycles repeat, teams often have no space to recover, review or refine. They stay stuck in reactive mode, despite their best efforts to plan ahead.

Cognitive periodisation offers a more sustainable model — one that respects the predictable patterns of finance work while creating space to manage the unexpected. It encourages teams to operate in cycles, with periods of deep focus followed by recovery and recalibration.

Here's how periodisation can look across the finance calendar:

- *Month-end reporting:* High-performance weeks. Eliminate distractions. Prioritise focused execution. These are delivery-heavy periods, where cognitive load is highest.

- *Post–month-end recovery:* Implement shorter meetings, lighter workloads and time for reflection. This is where clarity returns and burnout is prevented.

- *Quarterly reviews:* These require a transition phase. Use the lead-up for strategic prep rather than last-minute scrambling. With proper planning, quarterly reviews become insight-driven, and not just compliance exercises.

- *Year-end (EOFY or calendar year):* This is the marathon. After these periods, leaders should plan recovery through staggered leave, celebration and lighter expectations. Performance demands decompression to remain sustainable.

- *Mid-cycle windows:* These are conditioning phases. Use them for system improvements, training and strategic projects. These windows are where long-term value is built.

When finance leaders implement cognitive periodisation, they empower their teams to deliver with consistency without sacrificing health or long-term capability. Saying 'no' becomes strategic. Recovery becomes a priority. And planning becomes focused on performance rather than deadlines.

Because high-performing finance teams aren't just accurate—they're also resilient, focused and future-ready.

Project teams: From overlapping chaos to reflective execution

Project teams, especially in construction, infrastructure and home building, are designed to deliver results. In theory, they operate with structure, scoping, planning, executing and closing out in a clear sequence. Frameworks such as PMBOK, PRINCE2 and Agile all promote regular checkpoints, reviews and lessons learned.

On the ground, however, the rhythm often vanishes.

Rather than working on one job, most project teams are balancing two, three, or more. Deadlines clash, clients apply pressure and variations come through late. Staff move across sites mid-project. As one job blurs into the next, the structured pause for review is usually skipped.

I once asked a project manager overseeing residential builds whether he'd completed the project review. He said, 'No time. We're already into the next one.'

That particular project had faced repeated issues, including unreliable subcontractors, quality defects and avoidable rework. Yet nothing was being captured or corrected. When I asked him how he would avoid using those subbies again, he shrugged. 'We just have to keep going. The next client's already behind.'

Without time to reflect and a structured debrief, mistakes are repeated and teams push forward, frustrated and fatigued.

Cognitive periodisation helps project teams implement a rhythm that works, shifting from chaotic delivery to thoughtful execution by aligning energy, focus and planning across the full project lifecycle.

Here's how the four phases can apply for project teams:

1. *Pre-start—Conditioning Phase:* Before any site activity begins:

    - clarify project goals and what success looks like

    - define roles, responsibilities and decision-making structures

    - set communication norms and meeting rhythms

    - align stakeholders on process and priorities

    - use tools such as DiSC personality assessments (see www .discprofile.com for more information) to strengthen team awareness.

   This phase creates alignment and psychological safety before the pressure hits.

2. *Pre-mobilisation—Transition Phase:* Often rushed or skipped, this is the moment to gear up with the following:

    - finalise procurement and schedules

    - confirm site readiness and contractor availability

    - align expectations and risk mitigation plans.

   This phase shifts the team from preparation mode into execution, ensuring everyone starts in sync.

3. *Delivery—Performance Phase:* Instead of treating delivery like one long sprint, break it into the following peaks and recoveries:

    - anticipate milestones such as concrete pours or inspections

    - follow high-intensity periods with lighter weeks

    - run mini-reviews to check alignment and course-correct early.

   This prevents burnout and maintains clarity throughout.

4. *Close-out—Recovery Phase:* Don't rush this final stage; instead, implement the following:

- handover properly to the client

- review contractor performance

- debrief the team: What worked? What didn't? What will we change?

- recognise team wins and the effort invested.

Capturing insights here stops you from carrying problems into the next job.

5. *Between projects — Reset Phase:* A brief pause of even a few days can make a difference through allowing teams to:

- decompress

- reconnect to purpose

- reset mentally before re-engaging.

When project teams adopt this rhythm, they not only complete jobs but also evolve with each one. Performance improves, rework reduces and culture shifts from reactive to intentional.

Because great project work isn't just about output — it's also about learning, recovering and coming back better each time.

How to implement periodisation for teams and organisations

More than just a personal productivity hack, periodisation is a team performance strategy. By mapping the natural rhythms of work — whether seasonal, fiscal or project-based — teams can begin to build a healthier, more effective operating rhythm, preventing burnout and unlocking better, more consistent performance across departments and organisations.

Implementing periodisation effectively requires mapping work cycles, aligning workloads and structuring recovery periods to maintain high output without exhausting employees. This is where transparency becomes critical. Leaders need to create visibility across the year, highlighting when the team will push, when it will recover and where flexibility must be built in. Recovery phases must be planned rather than apologised for. Just like in sport or the military, business leaders must understand that contingency planning isn't a luxury. It's insurance for their people.

Because when your team knows what's coming, they can prepare. When they feel the rhythm, they can perform. And when they're given space to recover, they can return stronger, more engaged and ready for what's next.

The following sections provide a step-by-step guide to integrating periodisation into your team or organisation.

Step 1: Map your team's work rhythm

Every organisation experiences natural fluctuations in workload. The key is recognising these patterns so you can plan proactively rather than reactively. Work through the following:

- *Analyse past work trends:* Look at the last 6 to 12 months and identify when workloads peak and when natural lulls occur.

- *Identify deadlines and key business drivers:* What are the mission-critical deadlines? When does your team typically feel under the most pressure?

- *Survey your team:* Ask employees when they feel most stressed, overworked or productive to spot patterns in perceived high-intensity versus low-intensity periods.

An example may be a marketing team that peaks in February, June and October with major campaigns. They can then use April and August for recovery and planning, aligning work with natural highs and lows.

Action step: Gather data from performance reports, employee surveys and workload tracking to pinpoint predictable cycles of high-intensity work, routine execution and recovery periods.

Step 2: Structure your team's operating rhythm

Once you have identified your team's work cycles, structure them into the four key phases of periodisation.

Phase 1: Conditioning (routine, focus, energy)

This is the preparation phase, where teams lay the foundation for high performance. Use this time for the following:

- *Strategic planning:* Define objectives, align stakeholders and set the roadmap.

- *Process refinement:* Optimise workflows, clarify roles and eliminate inefficiencies.

- *Skill development:* Invest in upskilling, training and knowledge-sharing.

A product team, for example, could spend the first month of a quarter refining feature priorities, gathering stakeholder input and setting technical specifications before development begins.

Action step: Schedule a dedicated planning window at the start of each quarter to align goals, refine processes and run targeted skill-building sessions that prepare the team for upcoming execution.

Phase 2: Transition (prioritise, streamline, prime)

The Transition Phase shifts teams from preparation to execution by focusing on clarity, efficiency and readiness through the following:

- *Prioritisation:* Focus on high-impact tasks that align with strategic goals.

- *Streamlining:* Eliminate distractions, automate routine work and improve team workflows.

- *Priming for execution:* Set expectations, finalise action plans and ensure teams are mentally and operationally ready.

An example here could be a finance team who streamlines month-end reporting by automating reconciliations, reducing unnecessary meetings and priming for the deadline by clarifying roles and responsibilities.

Action step: Before high-performance phases, eliminate non-essential work, delegate tasks and ensure teams are aligned to reduce last-minute chaos.

Phase 3: Performance (execute, sustain, regenerate)

This is the execution phase, where teams operate at peak performance. The key is sustaining output without exhaustion. Implement the following:

- *Execute:* Block distractions, structure work in deep-focus sprints and maintain momentum.

- *Sustain:* Manage workloads effectively to sustain effort over longer work cycles.

- *Regenerate during execution:* Integrate short breaks and energy resets to avoid cognitive fatigue.

A sales team in the final two weeks of the quarter, for example, could focus exclusively on closing deals, eliminating all non-revenue-generating tasks and minimising unnecessary meetings.

Action step: Schedule deep-work blocks, focused execution sprints and tactical recovery to sustain performance throughout this phase.

Phase 4: Recovery (reset, recharge, rebuild)

Once major deadlines are met, teams must recover to rebuild energy and prepare for the next cycle. Have the following in place:

- *Reset:* Allow employees to step away and fully detach from work.

- *Recharge:* Encourage active recovery through movement, wellness initiatives and personal development.

- *Rebuild:* Conduct structured post-mortems, gather insights and refine strategies for the next performance cycle.

An example could be a marketing team who, after completing a high-stakes campaign, takes a week to reset, followed by a reflection session to evaluate what worked and what needs to improve.

Action step: Schedule team-wide recovery after major performance cycles, integrating downtime, flexible work periods and structured debriefs.

Step 3: Align the rhythm to people

Not everyone in your organisation operates on the same schedule, and aligning workloads ensures employees perform at their best without burnout. Here's how to take individual needs into account:

- *Match workloads to energy levels:* Identify when individual employees do their best work and schedule deep work accordingly.

- *Balance high and low cognitive load:* Assign deep work during performance phases and low-intensity work during recovery periods.

- *Identify peak performers and support roles:* Leaders, strategists and high-energy performers may take the lead in performance phases, while others can focus on execution and refinement.

A software engineering team, for example, could schedule complex coding tasks for mornings when developers are most focused, while reserving afternoons for meetings and admin work.

Action step: Meet with team leads and department heads to ensure everyone's workload aligns with their natural energy and cognitive cycles.

Step 4: Communicate the rhythm and adapt in real time

Periodisation is a dynamic strategy that needs to be communicated clearly and refined regularly. Here's how:

- *Set clear expectations:* Ensure teams understand their cycles and how workload allocation will improve performance and wellbeing.

- *Build cross-department alignment:* HR, sales, finance and product teams must be on the same page for company-wide periodisation to work.

- *Quarterly check-ins and adjustments:* What's working? What needs refinement? Use team feedback and performance metrics to tweak your approach.

For example, a customer success team could share their quarterly rhythm calendar with the sales and product teams, highlighting peak onboarding periods and planned recovery weeks. Regular check-ins could then help adjust workloads based on client demand and team capacity.

Action step: Schedule quarterly team reviews to assess workload balance, burnout risk and productivity trends, and then make data-driven adjustments.

Remember — periodisation isn't about going soft but about going smart. It's how elite teams sustain performance over time. If you want your team to not just survive but also thrive, this is your blueprint.

Tara's digital product team transformation

Tara was a digital product manager in a high-pressure government department responsible for rolling out critical online services to the public. Her team operated in quarterly cycles, managing tight deadlines, high stakeholder expectations and public scrutiny. While projects were delivered, the process was chaotic, with each quarter ending in a frantic sprint of last-minute fixes, rushed approvals and exhausted employees.

Despite their hard work, the team was running on fumes. Burnout was high, morale was low and productivity fluctuated wildly. It was clear that the team needed a structured, sustainable way to maintain performance without exhaustion. That's when Tara and I started working together.

Rather than treating each quarter as a flat-out race, we restructured it using the four key phases of cognitive periodisation.

(continued)

Conditioning: Laying the foundation for success

The first thing I worked on with Tara was shifting the team's mindset from survival mode to structured, high-performance execution. Rather than diving straight into development, we redesigned the first month of each quarter as a preparation phase to build a strong foundation. We focused on the following:

- *Clarifying priorities:* We worked closely with stakeholders to define clear objectives and high-impact features. This ensured the team had alignment from the start, preventing unnecessary rework later.

- *Optimising workflows:* We streamlined project management, introducing structured deep-work blocks to eliminate distractions. Unnecessary meetings were cut, and team-wide focus periods were implemented.

- *Protecting energy:* Tara and I designed workload pacing strategies, ensuring team members didn't burn out in the first few weeks. A realistic workload meant sustainable execution.

This phase shifted the team from reactive chaos to proactive planning, ensuring they entered the Performance Phase with clarity and confidence.

Transition: Structuring the work for maximum impact

Once the foundation was set, we turned our focus to how work was executed throughout the quarter. Tara's team needed a structure that reduced overwhelm while maintaining efficiency through the following:

- *Prioritising high-impact work:* We identified the 20 per cent of work that would drive 80 per cent of the impact, ensuring the most valuable tasks were tackled first.

- *Streamlining workload and minimising disruptions:* By introducing asynchronous updates and scheduled review sessions, we cut unnecessary meetings and maximised focused execution time.

- *Priming for high-stakes moments:* Instead of dreading last-minute approvals, the team incorporated progressive testing cycles and stakeholder reviews early on, eliminating the need for rushed fixes at the end of the quarter.

These changes gave the team a clear game plan that ensured workloads were balanced, priorities were clear and disruptions were minimised.

Performance: Executing with precision (and without exhaustion)

With the right structure and priorities in place, we moved into optimising execution. The goal was to ensure the team performed at their peak without constantly pushing past their limits. We implemented the following:

- *Executing deep work:* Tara introduced designated focus blocks, where team-wide deep work was prioritised without interruptions. Productivity skyrocketed.

- *Sustainable work cycles:* Rather than pushing through exhaustion, the team worked in 90-minute sprints, followed by short recovery breaks. This helped sustain focus and prevent burnout.

- *Using regeneration as a performance tool:* Unlike before, where long hours were the norm, Tara enforced a no after-hours work policy, allowing the team to recharge between intense work sessions.

The work schedule still wasn't always perfect. At times, long hours were necessary, especially in the final weeks leading up to a major launch. However, the difference was that this was now the exception, rather than the norm. Because the team had eliminated distractions, cut wasted effort and optimised their workflow, they had more time to focus on meaningful work during the day, reducing the need for constant overtime.

Before these changes, long hours were a result of inefficiency. Now, when they did happen, they were targeted, deliberate and temporary rather than a chronic issue. The team knew they could push when needed, but they also knew recovery would follow.

Recovery: Preventing burnout and sustaining long-term success

Tara's biggest breakthrough was realising that sustained success requires structured recovery. Instead of finishing every quarter completely drained, we built the following intentional recovery cycles into the workflow:

- *Reset:* We designed the final two weeks of each quarter to include buffer time, allowing the team to review, refine, and close out work without stress.

(continued)

- *Recharge:* Instead of immediately diving into the next cycle, we encouraged lighter workloads, creative thinking sessions, active recovery for energy restoration and personal development to provide a mental reset.

- *Rebuild:* We implemented structured quarterly retrospectives, ensuring the team reflected on what worked, what didn't, and how to improve the next cycle.

By making recovery as important as execution, the team ended each quarter strong rather than exhausted, ensuring they entered the next cycle refreshed and ready.

The transformation: High-performance without burnout

Through cognitive periodisation, Tara transformed her high-stakes, high-stress team into a structured, sustainable high-performance unit. The results spoke for themselves:

- The team consistently delivered high-quality products on time and with fewer last-minute scrambles.

- Stakeholders noticed the improvement, praising the team's calm efficiency and proactive approach.

- Morale skyrocketed as employees felt valued, supported and engaged, rather than exhausted and overwhelmed.

- Productivity improved without increasing hours as working smarter, not harder, became the new norm.

The team still had intense deadlines, but they were no longer constantly drowning. Instead, they had a sustainable structure that allowed them to perform at their best without burning out.

By working together, Tara and I proved that success doesn't come from grinding harder; instead, it comes from working strategically, managing energy and building recovery into the workflow.

Her team not only survived each quarter but also thrived through it, cycle after cycle.

CHAPTER 9

Your next move: Becoming a Cognitive Athlete for life

When a world-class pianist walks on stage, the audience sees only the performance — the fluid movement of hands, the quiet confidence and the brilliance of each note ringing through the hall. It looks effortless, like magic. But behind that three-minute performance lies months of structured preparation, hours of daily practice, and years of building muscle memory and mental focus. What we applaud in that moment is not only talent but also deliberate training, recovery and refinement.

Equally as important as what the audience sees are the warm-up rituals before the performance, the strategic rest days between shows, the quiet reflection after each concert to review what worked and what didn't. A concert pianist prepares, paces themselves and devotes time to recovery. And, in doing so, they sustain excellence over decades, not just during performances.

This is the same approach you must bring to your cognitive performance — because your work deserves more than noise and pounded keys. It deserves to be a masterpiece.

This book has challenged the narrative that work has to be a game designed for machines — one that rewards output, punishes rest, and treats recovery like an indulgence instead of a requirement.

Instead, you've learned that a Cognitive Athlete is someone who trains their brain like elite performers train their bodies — someone who moves with rhythm, rather than relentlessness, and doesn't just survive each week but also learns to design their week for impact.

So now the question is how will you lead from here? Because this isn't the end of your journey. It's the reset before your next performance cycle. From here, you get to decide whether you continue operating like the old version of yourself, always on and always stretched, or whether you take what you've learned and apply it — not all at once and not perfectly, but deliberately.

Because Cognitive Athletes don't wait for the chaos to stop. They train for it, they recover from it and they perform through it, with rhythm, resilience and purpose.

Now it's your turn.

The shift from hard work to smart work

As stressed throughout this book, effort alone is not a sustainable strategy. High performers understand that success isn't about working more hours; it's about making every hour count. They don't just show up and grind through their workload. They train themselves to execute at their peak when it matters most and recover effectively to sustain long-term success.

This is the essence of the Cognitive Athlete mindset:

- Your brain is your most valuable asset; train it, protect it and optimise it.

- You don't rise to the occasion; you fall to the level of your preparation.

- Sustained high performance requires cycles of intense focus and deliberate recovery.

The following sections provide a summary of the main ideas and themes in this book.

Train for high performance

Elite athletes don't step into competition without preparation. They train relentlessly for the moment that matters. Rather than relying on adrenaline, they rely on systems, habits and rehearsed routines. That's what separates the hopefuls from the high-performing.

Cognitive Athletes apply the same mindset. They don't wing it on Monday morning or brace for every deadline in a panic. They prepare, rehearse and structure their weeks with intention, using the following techniques:

- They align important work with their cognitive peaks, not during times when they're tired, distracted or multitasking.

- They treat deep work like a skill — one that gets stronger the more it's practised.

- They mentally rehearse high-stakes moments, presentations, negotiations and difficult conversations so when the pressure's on, they don't freeze — they flow.

This is the shift from reacting to performing. It's not about trying harder but about preparing smarter. High performance becomes predictable, repeatable and far less stressful.

Manage energy, not just time

We've been taught to treat time like our most precious resource. But any professional who's stared blankly at their screen for two hours knows that time without energy is useless.

Energy is the true currency of performance.

Cognitive Athletes manage their days by their energy rather than their appointments. They design their schedules around when they feel most focused, not just when the meetings are booked, through the following:

- They stack deep-work sessions during peak energy windows, typically mid-morning or late afternoon.

- They take deliberate micro-breaks to avoid mental fatigue — using the time for stretching, walking, breathwork or even momentary detachment.

- They protect their mornings from email clutter and carve out space for focus instead of firefighting.

Would you rather have eight hours of scattered, low-value effort or four hours of deep, impactful progress? When you master your energy, you become sharper, more creative and far less reactive. You stay ahead of your work, and not buried beneath it.

Recovery is a strategy, not a luxury

Most people wait until they're broken before they rest. Cognitive Athletes flip that script and recover before the crash. They do so because they understand that recovery isn't an afterthought but a performance enhancer.

Here's how they prioritise recovery:

- They step back after big sprints — not just physically but also cognitively. No meetings. No mental load. Just space.

- They use active recovery techniques such as breathwork, movement, nature and play to reset their nervous system.

- They reflect. What worked? What didn't? What will we do differently next time?

Recovery is where insight happens. It's where you metabolise the work, reconnect to purpose and sharpen for the next performance phase.

The world doesn't reward those who run themselves into the ground. It rewards those who can keep showing up at their best, over and over again. And that's what Cognitive Athletes do. They train, perform and recover — on purpose.

What's next?

Knowledge without action is useless. The Cognitive Athlete framework only works if you implement it. But don't worry — you don't need to overhaul your entire life overnight. Start small, be consistent and build momentum.

Here's how to take what you've learned in this book and put it into practice.

Choose one area to focus on first

Trying to change everything at once leads to frustration and failure. Instead, pick one phase of periodisation to focus on first. Select from the following:

- *Conditioning Phase:* If you're constantly overwhelmed, start by building foundational habits such as better sleep, structured exercise and focused work routines.

- *Transition Phase:* If your workload feels chaotic, prioritise what truly matters, streamline distractions and implement a structured weekly rhythm.

- *Performance Phase:* If you struggle with execution, refine your deep-work cycles, align tasks with energy peaks and protect focus time.

- *Recovery Phase:* If burnout is creeping in, schedule time off now, not when it's too late. Learn to reset, recharge and rebuild regularly.

Action step: Choose one phase and set a 30-day challenge to implement one small but meaningful change in that area.

Build your own periodisation plan

Success doesn't happen by accident but by design. Map out your own performance cycles using these steps:

- *Identify your natural work cycles:* When are your busiest and slowest periods? Align your deep work and recovery accordingly.

- *Schedule performance windows:* Plan high-focus work during peak cognitive hours.

- *Plan for recovery:* Schedule breaks, not just work, daily, weekly and quarterly.

- *Check-in and adjust:* Review what's working and refine it regularly.

Action step: Open your calendar and schedule your next performance and recovery cycle, even if it's just a small adjustment to your current routine.

Use the tools and resources that work for you

Not everyone thrives using the same methods. Find the tools that help you stay on track and use them. Consider the following:

- *Digital tracking tools:* Apps such as Notion, Todoist or Trello can help organise your deep work and recovery cycles.

- *Journaling and reflection:* A simple habit of reviewing your week can help you refine your system.

- *Accountability:* Share your plan with a colleague, mentor or coach to stay committed.

Action step: Pick one tracking method and use it for the next month.

Keep refining and evolving

High performance isn't a one-time effort; it's an ongoing practice. Even the best athletes and professionals refine their approach season after season. You'll have times when you lose momentum, fall into bad habits or feel stuck. That's normal. What matters is your ability to pause, reflect and reset. Ask yourself:

- What worked?

- What didn't?

- What needs to change in the next cycle?

Action step: Set a quarterly reminder to reflect and adjust your periodisation plan.

CONCLUSION

The Cognitive Athlete mindset: A lifelong journey

Being a Cognitive Athlete isn't about perfection. It's not about never feeling tired, always being focused or executing flawlessly every day. Instead, this approach is about consistency over intensity, and refinement over reinvention.

It's about showing up with intention, noticing when things start to drift and adjusting your rhythm before burnout takes hold. It's about designing your days with purpose, so you perform not only at a high level but also in a way that's sustainable, repeatable and human.

Remember—the real edge isn't found in a single sprint but in the cycle. Sustainable high performance comes from your ability to condition, perform, recover and then come back stronger.

So ask yourself:

- Are you working by default or by design?

- Are you pushing harder or leading smarter?

- Are you grinding through or building something that lasts?

You now have the tools, the framework and the mindset. All that's left is to begin. Start small and stay consistent. Refine as you go. Remember that you're not here to hammer out notes in a frenzy of activity. You're here to create something with rhythm, power and presence.

Like a master pianist, your performance is less about constant speed and more about control. It's about knowing when to pause, when to build and when to strike the final chord with confidence. This kind of intentional performance is the art of the Cognitive Athlete.

You can train with purpose, recover without guilt and keep refining your rhythm until the whole thing sings.

Your next cycle begins now.

Acknowledgements

To all my military colleagues I've had the privilege to serve with, each of you should write a book. We've shared stories and adventures that deserve to be told ... well, maybe not all the stories. The experiences, challenges and lessons we've lived through hold so much richness that others could truly benefit from reading about — though a few are probably best left in the mess, or at least off the record.

To my clients — thank you for trusting me to work alongside you. Your commitment, growth and successes have given me the confidence to write *The Cognitive Athlete*. Much of what fills these pages has been inspired by your journeys, and I'm grateful for the opportunity to learn with you and from you.

A huge thank you to Kelly Irving and the Expert Author Community, who have been a constant source of inspiration and support. Having a group to lean on and share ideas and thoughts with made this journey not only possible but enjoyable. Your feedback has been invaluable, and I'd recommend to anyone with an idea to put it down on paper and find a community like this to help bring it to life.

And to the Wiley team — thank you for giving me the opportunity to bring this book to life and thanks to Charlotte whose edits helped shape the book with greater clarity and a more natural, conversational tone.

Finally, to everyone who has encouraged, supported, or cheered me on along the way — thank you. This book is as much yours as it is mine.

References and further reading

Anton, NE, et al (2021), 'Surgeon stress negatively affects their non-technical skills in the operating room', *The American Journal of Surgery*, 222(6) 1154–57.

Arnsten, AFT (2009), 'Stress signalling pathways that impair prefrontal cortex structure and function', *Nature Reviews Neuroscience*, 10(6), 410–22.

Asurion (2022), 'The new normal: Phone use is up nearly 4-fold since 2019, according to tech care company Asurion', Asurion.

Baird, B, Smallwood, J & Schooler, JW (2011), 'Back to the future: Autobiographical planning and the functionality of mind-wandering', *Consciousness and Cognition*, 20(4), 1604–11.

Bangsbo, J, Mohr, M & Krustrup, P (2006), 'Physical and metabolic demands of training and match-play in the elite football player', *Journal of Sports Sciences*, 24(7), 665–74.

Baumeister, RF & Tierney, J (2011), *Willpower: Rediscovering the Greatest Human Strength*, Penguin Books.

Baumeister, RF, et al (1998), 'Ego depletion: Is the active self a limited resource?', *Journal of Personality and Social Psychology*, 74(5), 1252–65.

Bhatt, J, Fisher, J & Bordeaux, C (2023), 'The workforce well-being imperative: Paving the way for human sustainability in workplace culture', Deloitte Insights.

Boksem, MA, Meijman, TF & Lorist, MM (2005), 'Effects of mental fatigue on attention: An ERP study', *Cognitive Brain Research*, 25(1), 107–16.

Burzynska, AZ, et al (2017), 'The dancing brain: Structural and functional signatures of expert dance training', *Frontiers in Human Neuroscience*, 11, 566.

Chandola, T, et al (2008), 'Work stress and coronary heart disease: What are the mechanisms?', *European Heart Journal*, 29(5), 640–48.

Cohn, PJ (1991), 'An exploratory study on peak performance in golf', *The Sport Psychologist*, 5(1), 1–14.

Cranston, S & Keller, S (2013), 'Increasing the "meaning quotient" of work', McKinsey Quarterly.

Csikszentmihalyi, M (1990), *Flow: The Psychology of Optimal Experience*, Harper Perennial Modern Classics.

Danziger, S, Levav, J & Avnaim-Pesso, L (2011), 'Extraneous factors in judicial decisions', *Proceedings of the National Academy of Sciences*, 108(17), 6889–92.

Derks, D & Bakker, AB (2012), 'Smartphone use, work–home interference, and burnout: A diary study on the role of recovery', *Applied Psychology*, 63(3), 411–40.

Dhabhar, FS (2014), 'Effects of stress on immune function: The good, the bad, and the beautiful', *Immunologic Research*, 58(2–3), 193–210.

Dinges, DF, et al (1997), 'Cumulative sleepiness, mood disturbance, and psychomotor vigilance performance decrements during a week of sleep restricted to 4–5 hours per night', *Sleep*, 20(4), 267–77.

Dinges, DF & Powell, JW (1985), 'Microcomputer analyses of performance on a portable, simple visual RT task during sustained operations', *Behavior Research Methods, Instruments, & Computers*, 17, 652–55.

Driskell, T, Sclafani, S & Driskell, J (2014), 'Reducing the effects of game day pressures through stress exposure training', *Journal of Sport Psychology in Action*, 5, 28–43.

Ekstrand, J, Waldén, M & Hägglund, M (2004), 'A congested football calendar and the wellbeing of players: Correlation between match exposure of European footballers before the World Cup 2002 and their injuries and performances during that World Cup', *British Journal of Sports Medicine*, 38(4), 493–97.

Ericsson, KA, Krampe, RT & Tesch-Römer, C (1993), 'The role of deliberate practice in the acquisition of expert performance', *Psychological Review*, 100(3), 363–406.

Gallup (2020), *Gallup's Perspective on Employee Burnout: Causes and Cures*, Gallup, Inc.

Gallup (2022), 'Employee wellbeing is key for workplace productivity', Gallup, Inc.

Greenberg, N, et al (2003), 'Do military peacekeepers want to talk about their experiences? Perceived psychological support of UK military peacekeepers on return from deployment', *Journal of Mental Health*, 12(6), 565–73.

Guillot, A & Collet, C (2008), 'Construction of the motor imagery integrative model in sport: A review and theoretical investigation of motor imagery use', *International Review of Sport and Exercise Psychology*, 1(1), 31–44.

Hirshleifer, D & Teoh, SH (2003), 'Limited attention, information disclosure, and financial reporting', *Journal of Accounting and Economics*, 36(1–3), 337–86.

Howie, E (2023), 'Cognitive load management: An invaluable tool for safe and effective surgical training', *Journal of Surgical Education*, 80(3), 311–22.

Jackson, A (2024), 'What is the "let-down effect"? The reason you get sick on holiday', *Independent*, 19 January.

Kahneman, D (2011), *Thinking, Fast and Slow*, Farrar, Straus and Giroux.

Kaiser, D (2013), 'Infralow frequencies and ultradian rhythms', *Seminars in Pediatric Neurology*, 20(4), 242–45.

Khan, MA & Al-Jahdali, H (2023), 'The consequences of sleep deprivation on cognitive performance', *NeuroSciences (Riyadh)*, 28(2), 91–99.

Kleitman, N (1987), *Sleep and Wakefulness*, University of Chicago Press.

Leone, SS, et al (2008), 'A comparison of the course of burnout and prolonged fatigue: A 4-year prospective cohort study', *Journal of Psychosomatic Research*, 65(1), 31–38.

Lim, J & Dinges, DF (2010), 'A meta-analysis of the impact of short-term sleep deprivation on cognitive variables', *Psychological Bulletin*, 136(3), 375–89.

Locke, EA & Latham, GP (2002), 'Building a practically useful theory of goal setting and task motivation: A 35-year odyssey', *American Psychologist*, 57(9), 705–17.

Loehr, J & Schwartz, T (2003), *The Power of Full Engagement: Managing Energy, Not Time, Is the Key to High Performance and Personal Renewal*, Free Press.

Mark, G, Gudith, D & Klocke, U (2008), 'The cost of interrupted work: More speed and stress', Conference on Human Factors in Computing Systems — Proceedings, 107–110.

McEwen, BS (2007), 'Physiology and neurobiology of stress and adaptation: Central role of the brain', *Physiological Reviews*, 87(3), 873–904.

McGonigal, K (2016), *The Upside of Stress: Why Stress Is Good for You, and How to Get Good at It*, Avery.

Microsoft (2023), *Work Trend Index Annual Report: Will AI Fix Work?* Microsoft.

Microsoft (2021), 'Research proves your brain needs breaks', Microsoft Human Factors Lab.

Murphy, M (2016), 'Interruptions at work are killing your productivity', *Forbes*.

Newport, C (2016), *Deep Work: Rules for Focused Success in a Distracted World*, Little Brown.

O'Dhaniel, A, et al (2015), 'Cognitive fatigue destabilizes economic decision making preferences and strategies', *PLOS ONE* 10(9).

Ophir, E, Nass, C & Wagner, AD (2009), 'Cognitive control in media multitaskers', *Proceedings of the National Academy of Sciences*, 106(37), 15583–87.

Oppezzo, M & Schwartz, DL (2014), 'Give your ideas some legs: The positive effect of walking on creative thinking', *Journal of Experimental Psychology: Learning, Memory, and Cognition*, 40(4), 1142–52.

Palmer, L, et al (2021), 'The evolution of post-traumatic stress disorder in the UK Armed Forces: Traumatic exposures in Iraq & Afghanistan and responses of distress (TRIAD study)', King's Centre for Military Health Research.

Peng, L & Xiong, W (2006), 'Investor attention, overconfidence and category learning', *Journal of Financial Economics*, 80(3), 563–602.

Porges, SW (2011), *The Polyvagal Theory: Neurophysiological Foundations of Emotions, Attachment, Communication, and Self-regulation*, W.W. Norton & Company.

Raichle, ME (2015), 'The brain's default mode network', *Annual Review of Neuroscience*, 38, 433–47.

Raichle, ME & Gusnard, DA (2002), 'Appraising the brain's energy budget', *Proceedings of the National Academy of Sciences*, 99(16), 10237–39.

Ratey, JJ & Hagerman, E (2008), *Spark: The Revolutionary New Science of Exercise and the Brain*, Little, Brown and Co.

Reynolds, AC & Banks, S (2010), 'Total sleep deprivation, chronic sleep restriction and sleep disruption', *Progress in Brain Research*, 185, 91–103.

Robbins, T (1992), *Awaken the Giant Within: How to Take Immediate Control of Your Mental, Emotional, Physical and Financial Destiny!*, Simon & Schuster.

Rosekind, MR, et al (1995), 'Alertness management: Strategic naps in operational settings', *Journal of Sleep Research*, 4(S2), 62–66.

Rossi, EL (1991), *The 20-Minute Break: Reduce Stress, Maximize Performance, Improve Health and Emotional Well-being Using the New Science of Ultradian Rhythms*, Zeig, Tucker & Co.

Salmon, P (2001), 'Effects of physical exercise on anxiety, depression, and sensitivity to stress: A unifying theory', *Clinical Psychology Review*, 21(1), 33–61.

Sandberg, S (2013), *Lean In: Women, Work, and the Will to Lead*, Random House UK.

Sapolsky, RM (2004), *Why Zebras Don't Get Ulcers: The Acclaimed Guide to Stress, Stress-Related Diseases, and Coping — Revised Edition*, Henry Holt and Company.

Schwartz, T & McCarthy, C (2007), 'Manage your energy, not your time', *Harvard Business Review*.

Segerstrom, SC & Miller, GE (2004), 'Psychological stress and the human immune system: A meta-analytic study of 30 years of inquiry', *Psychological Bulletin*, 130(4), 601–30.

Shaffer, F & Ginsberg, P (2017), 'An overview of heart rate variability metrics and norms', *Frontiers in Public Health*, 5, 258.

Smith, A (2002), 'Effects of caffeine on human behavior', *Food and Chemical Toxicology*, 40(9), 1243–55.

Sonnentag, S & Fritz, C (2015), 'Recovery from job stress: The stressor-detachment model as an integrative framework', *Journal of Organizational Behavior*, 36(S1), S72–S103.

Sonnentag, S (2003), 'Recovery, work engagement, and proactive behavior: A new look at the interface between nonwork and work', *Journal of Applied Psychology*, 88(3), 518–28.

Sonnentag, S (2012), 'Psychological detachment from work during leisure time: The benefits of mentally disengaging from work', *Current Directions in Psychological Science*, 21(2), 114–18.

Sonnentag, S, Binnewies, C & Mojza, EJ (2008), '"Did you have a nice evening?" A day-level study on recovery experiences, sleep, and affect', *Journal of Applied Psychology*, 93(3), 674–84.

Spiegel, K, Leproult, R & Cauter, EV (1999), 'Impact of sleep debt on metabolic and endocrine function', *The Lancet*, 354(9188), 1435–39.

Steward, G, Looi, V & Chib, VS (2025), 'The neurobiology of cognitive fatigue and its influence on effort-based choice', *The Journal of Neuroscience*, 45(24).

Stickgold, R & Walker, MP (2007), 'Sleep-dependent memory consolidation and reconsolidation', *Sleep Medicine*, 8(4), 331–43.

Ströhle, A (2009), 'Physical activity, exercise, depression and anxiety disorders', *Journal of Neural Transmission*, 116(6), 777–84.

Sullenberger, C with Zaslow, J (2009), *Highest Duty: My Search for What Really Matters*, William Morrow & Company.

Summer, JV (2023), 'What is a NASA nap: How to power nap like an astronaut', www.sleepfoundation.org.

Sweller, J (1988), 'Cognitive load during problem solving: Effects on learning', *Cognitive Science*, 12(2), 257–85.

Sweller, J, et al (1998), 'Cognitive architecture and instructional design', *Educational Psychology Review*, 10(3), 251–96.

Syrek, CJ, et al (2018), 'Zeigarnik's sleepless nights: How unfinished tasks at the end of the week impair employee sleep on the weekend through rumination', *Journal of Occupational Health Psychology*, 23(2), 225–38.

Taylor, J & Wilson, G (eds) (2005), *Applying Sport Psychology: Four Perspectives*, Human Kinetics.

Teigen, KH (1994), 'Yerkes-Dodson: A law for all seasons', *Theory & Psychology*, 4(4), 525–47.

Thomas, C, Hertzman, C & Power, C (2009), 'Night work, long working hours, psychosocial work stress and cortisol secretion in mid-life; Evidence from a British birth cohort', *Occupational and Environmental Medicine*, 66(12), 824–31.

Treanor, J (2014), 'António Horta-Osório: "I nearly died — and it changed me"', *The Guardian*.

Ursin, H & Eriksen, HR (2004), 'The cognitive activation theory of stress', *Psychoneuroendocrinology*, 29(5), 567–92.

Van Dongen, HPA, et al (2003), 'The cumulative cost of additional wakefulness: Dose-response effects on neurobehavioral functions and sleep physiology from chronic sleep restriction and total sleep deprivation', *Sleep*, 26(2), 117–26.

Venkatraman, V, Huettel, SA & Chuah, YML (2015), 'Sleep deprivation biases the neural mechanisms underlying economic preferences', *Journal of Neuroscience*, 31(10), 3712–18.

Virtanen, M, et al (2009), 'Long working hours and cognitive function', *American Journal of Epidemiology*, 169(5), 596–605.

Walker, M (2017), *Why We Sleep: The New Science of Sleep and Dreams*, Penguin UK.

Walker, MP (2009), 'The role of sleep in cognition and emotion', *Annals of the New York Academy of Sciences*, 1156, 168–97.

Weick, KE & Sutcliffe, KM (2007), *Managing the Unexpected: Resilient Performance in an Age of Uncertainty*, Jossey-Bass.

Weinschenk, S (2012), 'The true cost of multi-tasking: You could be losing up to 40% of your productivity', *Psychology Today*.

Wiehler, A, et al (2022), 'A neuro-metabolic account of why daylong cognitive work alters the control of economic decisions', *Current Biology*, 32(16), 3564–75.

Wigert, B & Agrawal, S (2018), 'Employee burnout, part 1: The 5 main causes', Gallup Workplace.

Xie, L, et al (2013), 'Sleep drives metabolite clearance from the adult brain', *Science*, 342(6156), 373–77.

Yerkes, RM & Dodson, JD (1908), 'The relation of strength of stimulus to rapidity of habit formation', *Journal of Comparative Neurology & Psychology*, 18(5), 459–82.

Yoo, SS, et al (2007), 'A deficit in the ability to form new human memories without sleep', *Nature Neuroscience*, 10(3), 385–92.

Zheng, B, et al (2012), 'Workload assessment of surgeons: Correlation between NASA TLX and blinks', *Surgical Endoscopy*, 26(10), 2745–50.